Basic Fishing
A Beginner's Guide

Wade Bourne

Skyhorse Publishing

Skyhorse Publishing books may be purchased in bulk at special discounts for sales promotion, corporate gifts, fund-raising, or educational purposes. Special editions can also be created to specifications. For details, contact the Special Sales Department, Skyhorse Publishing, 307 West 36th Street, 11th Floor, New York, NY 10018or info@skyhorsepublishing.com.

Skyhorse® and Skyhorse Publishing® are registered trademarks of Skyhorse Publishing, Inc.®, a Delaware corporation.

Visit our website at www.skyhorsepublishing.com.

10 9

Library of Congress Cataloging-in-Publication Data is available on file.

Cover design by Adam Bozarth

Print ISBN: 978-1-63220-338-0
Ebook ISBN: 978-1-62636-920-7

Printed in China

PICTURE CREDITS

Larry Larsen: *Cover and title page;*
Duane Raver/USFWS: *14, 15, 16, 17, 18, 20, 21, 23, 24, 25;*
Timothy Knepp/USFWS: *18-19, 21, 22;*
Alex Bowers: *156*

Contents

Introduction /
Dedication

I have been an avid fisherman since I was old enough to hold a pole and watch a float bob on the water.

I was introduced to the sport by my father, Joe Bourne, who was one of the best crappie anglers I've ever known. More than 50 years ago, he and my uncle Doug built a wooden johnboat, and they powered it with an old 18-horse-power Johnson outboard. Together they used this rig to fish on nearby Kentucky Lake, which at the time was the largest manmade lake in the world.

They were smart fishermen. They figured out how to find and work sunken drop offs in the days before depth finders and electric trolling motors were in common use. My dad would sit backward in the bow of the boat, sculling with one hand and "tightlining" minnows along the drops with the other. It was sort of an "angler's ballet" – very coordinated, rhythmic and graceful. His "depth finder" was a heavy egg sinker tied to the end of his line. He used a fly rod to continuously lift and lower this sinker up and down off bottom. When it took longer to bump, he knew the bottom was deeper. If it bumped shorter, the bottom was shallower. In this way he could follow the old creek channel drops where the crappie were schooled. He and my uncle caught fish with amazing regularity!

My brother and I started going on these crappie trips when we were very young. My dad would rig us each a pole with a float, and we'd drag these behind the boat. We learned quickly that when our float disappeared, if we lifted quickly, we could hoist up a crappie.

I still remember the excitement of those trips, the fun we had, and the coolers full of "slabs" we'd bring home and clean for family fish fries. It was these early trips that instilled in me a love for fishing, its challenge, its rewards, and its simple good times. That love endures to this day.

My dad passed away in February, 2003. He was almost 88 years old. He left behind a legacy of exuberant good nature, caring for his family, and sharing his enthusiasm for fishing and hunting. Because he took the time to introduce my brother and me to the water and woods, we're both still avid sportsmen.

In fact, I turned this passion for the outdoors into a profession. I've been a full-time outdoor writer/broadcaster since 1979. In the process, I've had the pleasure of fishing some of the best waters with the best anglers in the world. I've caught everything from bluegill to giant tuna. I've shared my stories and shows with millions of anglers around the world. Still, some of my best memories are of those early days on the water with my dad and uncle and brother.

Today, I'm passing this love for the outdoors on to my children. My son is a "serious" fisherman and hunter. My daughter is less ardent about outdoor sports, but she still enjoys watching a float bob underwater and pulling out a sunfish. To each his or her own. That's the beauty of fishing and hunting. You can enjoy it at whatever level you wish – serious or casual.

Back in 1988 I wrote my first outdoor book, entitled *Fishing Fundamentals*. It was geared toward beginning anglers, and its purpose was to teach the basics of fishing. Moreover, my goal was to share the pleasures of fishing with others who had the desire, but not the know-how, to get into this sport. This book was very successful. It has been used by literally tens of thousands of anglers since it came out.

Basic Fishing covers much of the same information as that original book, and is updated to modern times. Most of the basic concepts of fishing are the same, but equipment has changed since 1988, and large technological advances have been made since then that help anglers increase their success and fun in fishing.

So, my fervent hope is that you apply the fishing instructions and strategies offered in the following pages and share in the fun. Fishing is truly an undertaking of joy, excitement, challenges and rewards. There is magic in dropping a bait in the water and pulling out a fish!

There are so many people to acknowledge and thank for their support of and contributions to this book. My wife Becky has been my love and my anchor over more than a quarter-century. She's the smartest, kindest, most fascinating woman I've ever met. My children, Hampton and Haley, are the best kids in the world. They bring true joy to their dad's heart. My mother has been the kind of mom all youngsters should have: loving, supportive and fun. My brother and I still join forces several times a year to pursue fish, ducks, turkeys and other critters. He's the perfect outdoor partner. I've also been blessed with fishing and business friends who are too numerous to mention. (One exception is Eddie Burchett, who put on his thinking cap and came up with the title for this book.)

I acknowledge my Creator for His soul-saving grace and love. It gives me pleasure to know that Jesus called fishermen from their boats to help in His earthly work.

In closing, I dedicate this book to my late father, Joe W. Bourne III. He is gone from this world, but never from my heart. Whatever heaven is like, I hope it includes a lake full of crappie and a creaky old johnboat so we can relive those early days of fishing together. I love you Pa, and I miss you.

WADE BOURNE

CHAPTER 1

Learn to Catch Fish — Guaranteed!

Fishing is a fun, healthy activity that anybody can enjoy. A catch like this mixed bag of saltwater fish will bring satisfaction to young and old anglers alike.

This book will teach you how to catch fish – guaranteed! This is true even if you've never fished before. Or, if you have some fishing experience, this book will help you increase your success. It will help you whether you fish from the bank or from a boat. It will help you if you're male or female, young or old, physically able or disabled. It doesn't matter. If you apply the instructions laid out in the following chapters, and you do so persistently, you will catch more fish and bigger fish. You will land more bass, bluegill, walleye, crappie, catfish, trout, etc., again – guaranteed!

How can I make this promise? I can do so because fishing is an undertaking of skill rather than luck. If you increase and sharpen

Fishing is enjoyed by more than 34 million Americans each year and most is done on quiet, out-of-the-way waters, either alone or in small groups. Fishing might lack the "high profile" of team sports, but it is one of the most popular recreational activities in America.

your skills, you will be more successful. Sure, luck sometimes plays a big role in fishing, but nobody's lucky all the time. But if you learn about fish and their habits; if you know where to find fish; if you know how to pick the right tackle and baits; and if you learn how to present these baits so they look natural and inviting to the fish; then your odds of success go way up. When skill starts replacing luck in your fishing outings, your catch rate will certainly begin to rise.

Thus, I can make this guarantee with complete confidence that – once

again – if you follow the instructions in this book, your fishing trips will be more productive.

There is an old saying in fishing that 10 percent of the anglers catch 90 percent of the fish. The reverse of this is that 90 percent of the anglers combine to catch only 10 percent of all fish taken on hook and line. The number of experts is small, while the number of beginners and mid-level fishermen is very large. Chances are, if you're reading this book, you are in the 90 percent group, and will profit from the following basic fishing instruction.

Even if you're an accomplished fisherman, it never hurts to go back and review the fundamentals. Sometimes the simplest oversight can cause an otherwise-sound fishing plan to fail. Coaches in all sports start with the basics, and they build successful programs on this foundation.

That's the game plan for Basic Fishing. We'll start with the basics: fish's nature and habits, where to find fish, selecting tackle and fishing accessories, tying rigs, and choosing baits. Then we'll progress to simple techniques for catching fish from ponds, lakes, streams and rivers. Finally, we'll go beyond the basics and cover such subjects as playing and handling fish, simple boats and motors, what to do when fish don't bite, how to build on your fishing skills, and fishing safety.

By the end of this book, if you put the instructions into practice, you will have advanced to a mid-level degree of proficiency, and you'll be able to take advantage of other, more advanced instructional material.

Why Get Into Fishing?

However, before getting started, why get into fishing? What will you gain by taking up this sport? There are many answers to these questions, because fishing offers different benefits to different people.

For most, it's a healthy, fresh-air activity that can be enjoyed by anybody. Fishing is no discriminator of age, sex or physical skills. Anyone who makes the effort can find a place and a way to catch fish, and experience the pleasures therein!

Fishing provides a perfect setting for fun and togetherness with family and friends. It's amazing how fishing removes barriers between people and allows them to understand and enjoy each other. Fishing is an especially good way for parents to build a strong relationship with children.

Fishing is a good way to make friends. Anglers share a mutual bond and speak a universal language. When two fishermen meet for the first time, they have something in common to talk about.

Fishing is a good way to get back to nature. On the water, the pressures of modern life seem to drift away on the breeze. It's a great way to relax, to tune into the soul-soothing rhythms of the wind and waves.

Fishing offers suspense and excitement. There's great drama in watching a bobber disappear

Successful fishermen depend on skill instead of luck. Basic Fishing *will teach you the basics you need to consistently make catches like this beautiful smallmouth bass.*

underwater, setting the hook, then battling the fish up to the bank or boat. When you catch a fish, you feel the excitement of a job well done. Fishing provides feelings of accomplishment and self-esteem as you learn the tricks of the sport and how to apply them successfully.

Fishing teaches patience. It teaches perseverance and how to work toward goals. Ponds, lakes and streams can be natural classrooms for some very important lessons in life.

And last, fishing can be a source of nutritious, delicious-tasting food. There are few banquets as pleasing as fresh fish that you've caught, cleaned and cooked.

However, there is a warning that should be given regarding this sport! With all its benefits, fishing also carries certain liabilities. It'll hook you just like you plan to hook the fish. It'll cause you to crawl out of bed well before sunrise, travel long distances, burn enormous amounts of energy, and even spend large sums of money, all for the chance of tricking a simple fish into biting a bait. For many, fishing is truly addictive.

Understand, though, that you don't have to go to these extremes to catch fish. You can make this sport what you want it to be. It's not all hardship and effort and expense. If you so choose, it can be laid back and inexpensive, close to home and unsophisticated. This is one of the beauties of fishing. You certainly don't need a fancy boat, expensive tackle and baits, and the intelligence of Einstein to catch fish. You can keep this sport simple, or challenging. You decide!

Master Plan for Fishing

My guess is that you fall into one of two categories: (1) you've never tried fishing before, and you want to learn; or (2) you go fishing occasionally, and you'd like to improve your success. In either case, this book will guide you step-by-step toward achieving your goal.

First, I will explain the master plan we'll follow as you learn to fish. It's important to be methodical and to keep this process in the right order. We'll start with the basics – learning about fish, where to fish, tackle, rigs, baits, and simple fishing techniques. Then we'll progress beyond these basics to round out your education. My goal is to take you from "point zero" to where you have a real ability to find and catch fish.

Anybody can be successful at fishing: female or male, young or old, athletic or infirm. The key is to learn basic skills and to apply them in waters where fish are both plentiful and available.

However, before going too far, let's take a brief look at the world of fishing and the people who participate in it.

A Look at the World of Fishing

Some 34 million Americans go fishing at least once a year, and many of these go numerous times. These people fish a total of 557 million days a year. They spend a combined $36 billion annually and would rank 40th on the Fortune

500 list. The fishing industry supports a million jobs (more than the combined totals of Exxon-Mobil, Ford and GMC). Five million more Americans fish than play golf. The number of sportsmen (anglers and hunters) could fill every NFL and Major League Baseball stadium six times over. In a year, sportsmen generate over six times more revenue than Hollywood's top 40 movies of all time. Truly, fishing and hunting are high-profile sports.

However, fishing doesn't get the exposure of the big team sports. Most fishermen participate alone or in small groups, without scores and cheerleaders, on out-of-the-way waters scattered across the continent. On any weekend, North America's ponds, lakes, streams and rivers are dotted with bank and boat anglers who quietly seek their own pleasures. (True, big-time tournaments are a growing phenomenon in fishing, but the number of tournament anglers remains small in comparison to anglers who fish for fun or food.)

There are two reasons for this large number of fishermen. There are more people and more fishing possibilities than ever before. In recent decades, hundreds of reservoirs have been built throughout the U. S. and Canada. At the same time, fisheries biologists have learned more about managing fish and stocking species into waters where they weren't previously found. Water quality laws have transformed formally-polluted waters into places with thriving fish populations. Quite literally, new fishing opportunities have been created from east to west.

Fishing bridges the gap between people of all educational and economic levels. Several U. S. presidents have been avid fishermen, including Herbert Hoover, Franklin D. Roosevelt, Harry Truman, Dwight Eisenhower, Jimmy Carter, George Bush, and George W. Bush. Hoover once described fishing as "a discipline in the equality of man, for all men are equal before fish." Grandparents, parents and children are peers in this sport. Recent research shows large increases in the number of senior citizens and single parents who have taken up fishing.

Each year the fishing tackle industry turns out increasingly better rods, reels, line, lures and accessories. Today anglers can purchase electronic accessories that do everything from taking water temperature to a giving satellite "fix" on location. Researchers are

Learning to fish is a matter of figuring out where the fish are, what they're doing and what bait they'll hit. Then you offer a logical bait in the most efficient and appealing manner possible. The rest is up to the fish.

learning more about fish – where they live, what they eat, and how they react to different stimuli in their watery world.

Some fishermen feel these gadgets and research findings take some of the mystery away from the sport. They decry the substitution of technology for plain old fishing know-how. I disagree with

this, however, for one reason. We still don't have a way to make fish bite when they don't want to, and until we do, fishing will retain its elements of uncertainty and chance. But I also agree with a friend who says, "I hope we never learn all there is to know about fish." As long as we don't, the mystery and anticipation in fishing will remain.

Meanwhile, all the information and new gear will make it easier for you to learn to fish. They will reduce the amount of time it will take you to gain proficiency. You don't have to learn old trial-and-error lessons on the water. There are many shortcuts available to help in your fishing apprenticeship, and I recommend that you take them.

In its most basic sense, learning to fish is a matter of stacking the odds in your favor: figuring out where the fish are, what they're doing and what bait they'll hit. Then you offer a logical bait in the most efficient and appealing manner possible. You do everything you can to make it easy for fish to bite, and from that point, it's up to the fish.

Sometimes they cooperate; sometimes they don't. But they will cooperate a lot more often if

Fishing provides a common bond between parents and children. It gives them something to plan, look forward to, and enjoy together.

you build your fishing around skill instead of luck. As I said, luck plays a big role in this sport, but good fishermen will almost always catch more fish than "lucky" fishermen.

Teaching Children to Fish

As I mentioned earlier, fishing is an excellent way for parents and children to spend time together. If more parents took their kids fishing, family bonds would be stronger, and inter-family problems would be fewer. Fishing gives kids something constructive to do, an activity to occupy their time. Fishing provides a common tie between parents and children. It gives them something to plan, look forward to, and enjoy together.

Parents should be careful how they introduce their children to fishing, however. Those first trips should be short, simple and with a maximum opportunity for catching such "easy" fish as sunfish, perch or bullheads. Don't start out fishing more than an hour or two. Don't get frustrated if your kids lose interest. Don't criticize them if they have trouble with their tackle. Don't nag them if they want to throw rocks in the water instead of sitting quietly and watching a bobber. Remember, fishing should be fun! If you make those first trips enjoyable, your kids will keep coming back. Then, before you know it, they'll get serious and you'll have fishing partners for life.

The Concept of Structure

As you undertake the following study course on fishing, one concept will appear over and over in regards to locating fish and catching them: the concept of STRUCTURE. I've capitalized this word for emphasis. This is the key to finding fish, which is the first step in getting them to bite.

Here's the idea. Most fish don't just meander randomly through their home water. Instead, they hang around specific, predictable spots most of the time. These are places that have some difference or feature that the fish like or use in their daily lives. In fishing, these differences or features are called "structure."

Let's use a simple example to explain this concept. Say there's a man walking in a desert. If there's nothing but sand, he'll wander aimlessly. But if somebody erects a telephone pole in the middle of that desert, he'll walk straight to it and probably hang around it. The telephone pole gives him a point of

reference. Or, say somebody builds a fence across the desert, and the man encounters it. He'll probably turn and follow it. Now he has something to give order to his movements. If the telephone pole I mentioned is somewhere along the

By learning and applying fishing's basics, anybody can achieve success in this sport.

fence, this is a likely spot for the man to stop, since this place is different, hence more attractive, compared to the rest of the desert.

Underwater features affect fish the same way. If the bottom is flat and void of any special features, fish will swim around without any pattern. But there's almost always some structure that will attract or guide their movements. Submerged stumps, logs, rocks, weed clumps and other objects are like the telephone pole. They give fish something to orient to. A sunken creek or river channel, a submerged gully or an inundated roadbed is like the fence. Fish will swim along it. A stump or rockpile on the edge of a sunken channel or a bend in the channel is a likely place for a fish to stop and rest as it swims along this structure.

As we proceed into succeeding chapters, remember that structure is anything different from the norm. This applies to ponds, natural lakes, manmade reservoirs, streams and rivers - wherever fish live. Structure can be sunken channels, reefs, bridge foundations, boat docks, manmade fish attractors, an old car sunk in the lake, or anything different from a clean, smooth bottom.

The sunfish is one of North America's most available, most popular species. Basic Fishing *teaches simple techniques for catching this and other freshwater species.*

Also, structure may be more subtle, such as a spot where the current changes direction; where there is a change in bottom makeup (for instance, where a mud bottom changes into gravel); where muddy water gives way to clear; or even where shadows fall onto the water's surface.

The point is, think changes or differences in the fish's environment,

Tree stumps, their roots exposed by erosion, dot the shoreline of an impoundment lake. Most fish orient to "structure," which can be stumps, a sunken creek channel, or a rock ledge. When water rises over these stumps in springtime, they will be prime spots to catch crappie, bass or other species.

and you'll be thinking structure. In Chapter 8 we'll get into a more detailed discussion of how fish relate to structure and how this affects specific fishing techniques.

The Scope of *Basic Fishing*

Basic Fishing teaches methods for catching popular freshwater fish. It does not cover saltwater fish. While much of the information in the following chapters applies to saltwater fishing, this fishery is different in terms of species and techniques for catching them. Saltwater

fishing would be a good subject for another book.

Instead, Basic Fishing confines itself to traditional North American fishing found in freshwater lakes, reservoirs, streams and rivers. This book covers species that are the most likely targets of entry-level anglers, and it describes simple ways to catch them. Less popular species and more complicated fishing methods have been omitted. In math, you have to learn to add before you can do algebra. In fishing, you have to master the basics before moving ahead to more difficult procedures. That is the focus of this book.

The following chapters contain these basics in an easy-to-follow sequence. Study them. Digest them. Then put them into practice. And remember that the more you fish, the better you'll understand this sport, and the more success you'll enjoy in it. If I were a "doctor of fishing" and you were my patient, I'd prescribe a concoction of water, fresh air, fishing tackle and baits. Mix well and take on a regular basis. I guarantee, this is one medicine that will go down easy!

CHAPTER 2

Popular Fish Species of
North America

LARGEMOUTH BASS

Fish are some of the most interesting creatures on earth! They come in an amazing variety of species and sizes. They live in virtually all waters where their life basics are available to them. Some are predators; they feed on other fish and aquatic creatures. Others are prey species, spending their lives in danger of being gobbled by larger fish that share their waters.

The first step in learning to catch fish is learning about fish: which species are available, where they can be found, and what they eat. The more you know about your target species' life habits, the more likely you are to catch them. Many expert anglers learn even the smallest details about the daily patterns of the fish they're after. This helps them locate the fish and select just the right bait and technique to make them bite.

Following is a brief look at the freshwater fish species that are most popular with North American anglers. As your fishing skills grow and you become more specialized, you should add to this knowledge until you have a broad understanding of where to find individual species and what to do to catch them under varying conditions.

Black Bass

Many authorities consider black bass to be the most important fish in North America. Actually, this group (genus Micropterus) includes three popular species: largemouth bass, smallmouth bass and spotted bass. These fish are closely related genetically, but they differ in the waters they prefer, favorite foods, spawning habits and other life basics.

The largemouth is the most abundant bass, and it grows larger than smallmouth or spotted bass. Largemouth live in natural lakes, reservoirs, rivers, streams and ponds from Mexico to Canada and from the East Coast to the West Coast. These fish normally feed and rest in quiet, relatively shallow water, and they like to hold around such cover as vegetation, rocks, logs, stumps, brush, etc.

As with many species, largemouth bass grow bigger in southern states where warmer weather provides a longer growing season. In Florida, Georgia, Texas, southern California, Mexico and other southern climes, largemouths over 15 pounds are occasionally boated. On the other hand, in northern states and Canadian provinces, largemouths over 7 pounds are rare. The world record largemouth bass was caught in south Georgia in 1932. It weighed 22 pounds 4 ounces.

Largemouth bass are predators that eat a wide range of foods. Their primary diet consists of baitfish, crawfish, frogs and insects, but they will also strike baby ducks, mice, snakes any virtually any other living creature that it can swallow.

SMALLMOUTH BASS

Smallmouth bass prefer clearer, cooler waters than largemouth. They like a rocky or sandy environment, and they adapt well to medium-strength currents. Because of these preferences, they thrive in streams, lakes and reservoirs of the Northeast, Midwest and southern Canadian provinces. Also, the Great Lakes support huge smallmouth populations. Smallmouth bass occur naturally as far south as north Alabama and Georgia, and they have been successfully stocked into lakes and rivers west of the Rockies. The world-record smallmouth was caught in Tennessee in 1969. It weighed 10 pounds 14 ounces.

BLUEGILL SUNFISH

Smallmouth bass are also feeding opportunists. Their favorite prey are minnows and crawfish, but they will also eat a wide variety of other foods when available.

Spotted bass (also called "Kentucky bass") are the third common member of the black bass family. For years this fish was confused with both largemouth and smallmouth bass, but it was recognized as a distinct species in 1927.

The spotted bass is something of an intermediate species between the largemouth and smallmouth both in appearance and habits. Its name comes from rows of small, dark spots running from head to tail below a lateral band of dark-green, diamond-shaped blotches. Spotted bass occur naturally from Texas to Georgia and north up the Mississippi, Ohio and Missouri River drainages. These fish have also been stocked in several western states. In fact, the current world record spotted bass (10 pounds 4 ounces) was caught in California in 2001.

Spotted bass like some current, but not too much. They like deep water, but not as deep as smallmouth prefer. They collect in large schools and chase baitfish in open water. They feed primarily on baitfish, crawfish and insects.

Some lakes contain all three of these black bass species. Largemouth will be back in the quiet coves. Smallmouth will hold along deep shorelines and main lake reefs; and spotted bass will roam through the open lake in search of prey. Sometimes these three bass species will mix to feed on the same food

BLACK CRAPPIE

source. However, more often each species stays in areas where it feels most comfortable.

Spawning habits of black bass species are similar. When water temperature approaches the mid- 50° F range, these fish all go on feeding binges to build up energy for the approaching egg-laying, hatching process. Smallmouth and spotted bass begin nesting when the water temperature approaches 60°. These fish usually establish their nests on main-lake shorelines or flats, frequently next to a stump, rock, log, etc. that offers some shelter. Largemouth prefer 65° water before spawning, and they will fan their nests in wind-protected areas along the sides or back of lake embayments. Largemouth typically nest in shallower water (2-5 feet on average) than smallmouth or spotted bass.

Sunfish

To biologists, "sunfish" is the family name for several species, including bass, crappie and bluegill. However, to most anglers, "sunfish" is a collective term for bluegill, shellcrackers (redear sunfish), pumpkin seeds, green sunfish, longear sunfish, warmouth and other similar species that southerners call "bream." These are the most numerous and widespread of all panfish. They are willing feeders, which makes them easy to catch. They're also scrappy fighters, and they're delicious to eat. This is why sunfish are extremely popular with beginning anglers. It's a safe bet that a sunfish was the first catch of the vast majority of North American fishermen.

Sunfish live in warm-water lakes, reservoirs, rivers and ponds throughout the U.S. and southern Canada. They spend most time in shallow to medium depths, usually around weeds, rocks, brush, boat docks or other cover types. They feed mostly on tiny invertebrates, larval and adult insects, worms, small minnows and other prey.

Sunfish are capable of reproducing in great numbers. One adult female will produce tens of thousands of eggs in a single season. Because of this, many smaller waters experience sunfish overpopulation. The result is lots of little

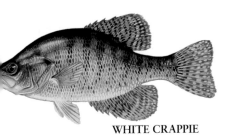

WHITE CRAPPIE

fish that never grow large enough to be considered "keepers" by fishermen. However, in waters where there are enough bass and other predators to prevent overpopulation, some sunfish species will average a half-pound in size, and some individuals can exceed a pound.

The bluegill is the most popular sunfish. The world-record bluegill was caught in Alabama in 1950. It weighed a whopping 4 pounds 12 ounces!

Crappie

Crappie are widespread and abundant in many waters, and they're prized for their delicious table quality. They average larger in size than sunfish, and they are fairly easy to catch. These are reasons why millions of anglers target these fish each year.

Actually, there are two crappie species: white and black. Differences between these species are minor. One apparent difference is as their names imply. Black

crappie have darker, blotchier scale patterns than white crappie, which usually have dark vertical bars.

Both these species live in natural lakes, reservoirs, larger ponds and quiet, deep pools of medium-to-large streams. Crappie occur naturally from southern Ontario to the Gulf of Mexico in the eastern half of North America. They, too, have been stocked into numerous lakes and rivers in the West. Black crappie are typically found in cooler, clearer lakes, while white crappie inhabit warmer lakes that are dingier in color.

Traditionally, most crappie fishing occurs in the spring, when these fish migrate into quiet, shallow areas to spawn. When the water temperature climbs into the low-60° F range, they begin laying eggs in or next to such cover as reeds, brush, stumps, or manmade fish attractors built and sunk by anglers.

After spawning, crappie head back to deeper water, where they collect in schools and hold along sunken creek channels, weedlines, standing timber, sunken brush piles and other areas where the lake bottom contour changes suddenly or where deep submerged cover exists. Expert crappie anglers know that these fish can be caught from such areas all year long, though they must employ some fairly specialized techniques to do so.

Crappie feed mainly on small baitfish and invertebrates. In some lakes, they average a pound or more in size; crappie over 2 pounds are considered trophies. The world-record white crappie weighed 5 pounds 3 ounces and was caught in Mississippi in 1957. The world-record black crappie weighed 4 pounds 8 ounces and was boated in Virginia in 1981.

Walleye

The walleye is a member of the perch family. It gets its name from its large, glassy, light-sensitive eyes. While walleye average 1-3 pounds, in some waters they grow to more than 20 pounds. Many walleye experts consider fish over 10 pounds to be trophies. The world-record walleye, weighing

an even 25 pounds, was caught in Tennessee in 1960.

Many anglers highly prize walleye for its table quality. Its meat is white, firm and mild-tasting. Because of this eating quality and its abundance in many waters, the walleye is a favorite among anglers wherever it's found.

Walleye are native to cool, clean lakes, reservoirs and major rivers of the central U. S. and much of Canada. They have also been stocked in both eastern and western waters outside their home range.

Walleye spend most of their time in deep main lake/ river areas where there is good water circulation, but they also frequently feed on shallow flats and close to shore. They normally move into these areas in low-light periods such as night, dawn, dusk, cloudy days or when vegetation or muddy water shields them from bright sunlight. A walleye's main food is small

WALLEYE

baitfish, though it will also feed on insects and small crustaceans and amphibians.

Walleye are early spawners. Their spawning run starts when the water temperature climbs above 45° F. Walleye in lakes spawn on shallow flats with hard, clean bottoms. In rivers, walleye spawn below riffles in pools with rock or sand bottoms. In river-fed lakes and reservoirs, and upstream spawning run is the rule. When spawning, one large female walleye can lay several hundred thousand eggs.

One characteristic of these fish is especially pertinent to beginning anglers: they have sharp teeth! Fishermen who stick a finger into a walleye's mouth will get a painful surprise. Instead, they should be gripped across the back.

Sauger

Sauger are closely related to walleye, and many people confuse them because of their similar appearance and habits. But there are two easy ways to tell them apart. Sauger have dark, saddle like blotches on their backs (as opposed to the walleye's smooth golden scale pattern). Also, sauger have dark spots on the main dorsal fin. (A walleye's dorsal fin is spot-free.)

SAUGER

Sauger don't grow as large as walleye; they seldom reach 4 lbs. (The world record sauger – 8 pounds 12 ounces – was caught in North Dakota in 1971.) The sauger is a river fish, though it also lives in river impoundments and some natural lakes. Its range includes the Mississippi Valley west of the Appalachian Mountains and north to James Bay in Canada. Sometimes sauger are found co-existing with walleye, but they're more tolerant of dingy water than walleye. This means sauger can thrive in slow-moving, silty streams where walleye can't survive.

The sauger's feeding and spawning habits are very similar to those of walleye. This fish is also prized by anglers for its fine table quality. And like walleye, sauger have sharp teeth which should be avoided by anglers.

Yellow Perch

Along with walleye and sauger, yellow perch are members of the perch family. These fish average 6-10 inches long, though many lakes

YELLOW PERCH

only have stunted "bait stealers" that are smaller than this average. Still, yellow perch are very popular since they are delicious to eat. The world-record yellow perch (4 pounds 3 ounces) was caught in New Jersey in 1865.

The yellow perch's natural range extends throughout the Northeast, Midwest and Canada (except British Columbia). It lives in all the Great Lakes and inhabits many brackish waters along the Atlantic Coast. Yellow perch have also been stocked in many reservoirs outside their natural range. These fish thrive in clean lakes, reservoirs, ponds and large rivers that have sand, rock or gravel bottoms. They also abound in weedy, mudbottomed lakes, though these are the type spots where they tend to run small in size.

Yellow perch swim in schools and feed on minnows, small crustaceans, snails, leeches and invertebrates. Adults spend most of their lives in deep water, usually moving shallow to feed, mostly during daylight hours in areas exposed to sunlight.

These fish begin spawning when the water temperature climbs into the mid-40° F range (mid- 50s in the southern part of their range). Yellow perch often make spawning runs up feeder streams; they also spawn around shallow weeds and brush.

Muskellunge

Many anglers view the "muskie" as the supreme freshwater trophy fish. Muskies are top-of-the-food- chain predators. They are never very numerous in any body of water. They grow huge in size. They're hard to get to bite, but when they do, they fight savagely. Muskie anglers often cast for hours or even days without getting a strike. When they finally do hook one of these fish, however, they experience one of the most difficult

MUSKELLUNGE

and exciting challenges in all of fishing. Muskies are the wild bulls of the water, and it takes great skill and dedication to land them consistently.

The muskie is a member of the pike family. It is found in natural lakes, reservoirs and streams/rivers in the Northeast, upper Midwest and southern Canada. This fish requires cool, clean water.

The muskie is cylinder-shaped, and it has a long, powerful body. Its sides are usually yellow tined and marked with dark blotches or bars. This fish has a flat, duck-like mouth and very sharp teeth! It feeds mainly on smaller fish, but it will also attack birds, small musk-rats and other hapless creatures that enter its domain.

Muskies typically stalk their prey alone in shallow water, around reeds, rocky shoals, quiet eddy pools in streams, and other similar spots. During warm months, they feed more in low-light periods of dawn and susk. On cloudy days, however, they may feed anytime. One of the very best times to fish for muskies is during fall when they go on a major pre-winter feeding binge.

Muskies live many years and frequently grow beyond 35 pounds. The current world record, weighing 67 pounds 4 ounces, was caught in Wisconsin in 1949.

Since the muskie is such a vicious predator, nature has a way of keeping its numbers down so other fish have a chance to sur-vive. The muskie is a late spawner (water temperature in the mid-50° F range). The fish that survive, however, grow to rule over their home waters. The only predator to big muskies is man.

Northern Pike

It would be fair to call pike the "poor man's muskie." Members of the pike family, "northerns" are much more numerous than muskies, and they are easier to catch. By nature, pike are very aggressive, and they often attack any bright, flashy lure that swims by.

Pike inhabit natural lakes, reservoirs, rivers and streams throughout the northeastern and north-central U. S. and most of Canada. They thrive in warm, shallow lakes or river sloughs with an abundance of water weeds.

The pike's body is shaped like a muskie's: long and round with the same flat, pointed mouth and sharp teeth. Its color is dark olive on the sides with light, wavy spots. Its belly is white. Pike can grow over 20 pounds. Because they're so vulnerable to fishing pressure, big ones are usually found only in lakes off the beaten path. The world-record pike (55 pounds 1 ounce) was caught in Germany in 1986.

Pike spawn in quiet, shallow areas when the water temperature climbs into the 40° F range. After spawning, they linger around weedbeds, especially those close to sharp underwater contour changes.

They are not school fish by nature, but they will cluster together if their food source is concentrated. Like muskies, they eat almost anything that swims, floats or dives. Most of the pike's diet consists of fish, and they will attack prey up to half their own body size.

When hooked, a pike is a strong battler, rolling on the surface and shaking its head from side to side. It isn't the most desirable table fish because of its many small bones, but anglers can learn to remove these bones during cleaning. The meat of the pike is white, flaky and tasty.

Pickerel

These toothy predators are a mini-version of pike and muskies. Their sides are covered with a yellowish chain pattern on a green background. They're aggressive strikers, and they give a good fight on light tackle. Most pickerel range from 1-3 pounds, but can grow larger than this in southern habitats. The world-record chain pickerel, caught in Georga in 1961, weighed 9 pounds 6 ounces.

The grass and redfin pickerels rarely reach a foot in length. The redfin is found along the Atlantic coastal plain in small creeks and

PIKE

CHAIN PICKEREL

shallow ponds. The grass pickerel's range is primarily in the Mississippi and Great Lakes drainages.

Pickerel spawn in shallow weeds as water temperatures reach the high 40° F range. Pickerel are active in cold water, and the best seasons for catching them are late fall, winter and spring. They feed primarily on small fish, so active lures like spinnerbaits, in-line spinners, spoons and floating minnow lures work well on them.

Trout

Several trout species inhabit North American waters and are very important sportfish. They live in many different types of waters, from small brooks to huge lakes. Some trout are natives; others are raised in hatcheries and released into suitable waters. Trout are coldwater fish and lively fighters when hooked. They have sweet, delicate meat. Because of their wide availability, natural elusiveness, fighting qualities and good flavor, these fish are highly sought by anglers.

The U. S. and Canada have five major trout species: rainbows, German browns, brook trout, cutthroats and lake trout. Six other species found in localized areas are Apache trout, Arctic char, bull trout, Dolly Vardens, Gila trout and golden trout.

Rainbows are so-named because of the pink streak down their sides. Native to western states, this fish has been stocked into streams, ponds and lakes throughout much of the U. S. and lower Canada. Today the rainbow trout is probably the continent's most important cold-water sportfish. The world record rainbow trout (42 pounds 2 ounces) was caught in Alaska in 1970.

The German brown trout is a European native that has been widely stocked in suitable American waters. These fish have dark or orange spots on their sides. Many anglers consider them to be the wariest, most difficult trout to catch, making them extremely popular among sport anglers. Browns

RAINBOW TROUT

LAKE TROUT

CUTTHROAT TROUT

tolerate slightly higher water temperatures than other trout, so they can live where some of the other trout can't. The world-record brown trout (40 pounds 4 ounces) was taken in Arkansas in 1992. (When the angler who caught this fish died, he had the taxidermy mount of his world-record brown buried with him.)

Brook trout are native to the eastern U. S. and Canada, though they have been transplanted into other areas. They have light, worm-like markings along their backs. They also have small blue and red dots along their sides. "Brookies" are probably the easiest of all trout to catch, and they are the best to eat. The world-record brook trout (14 pounds 8 ounces) was taken in Ontario in 1916.

Cutthroat trout are found mainly in the western U. S. and Canada. Their name comes from the red markings behind and under the lower jaw. Their sides are dotted with small black spots. Like brook trout, they are not too difficult to catch, and they're delicious to eat. The world-record cutthroat, weighing an even 41 pounds, was caught in Nevada in 1925.

Lake trout are what their name implies: residents of large, coldwater lakes from Canada south through the Canadian shield lakes of northern and Midwestern states. Lake trout also live in many western lakes where water temperatures don't exceed 65° F. Lake trout are silver- gray in color, and they have deeply-forked tails. The world-record lake trout weighed 72 pounds and was caught in Canada's Northwest Territories in 1995.

Trout feed on a broad variety of larval and adult insects, minnows, worms and crustaceans. In streams, trout spawn in shallow riffles where they build nests (or "redds") in gravel.

Salmon

Pacific salmon were first stocked into the Great Lakes in the late 1960s. Continued stockings have established an abundance of fishing opportunities for anglers in the Upper Midwest.

Chinook salmon is the largest species, reaching more than 30 pounds in some of the Great Lakes. (The world-record Chinook weighed 97 pounds 4 ounces and was caught in Alaska in 1985.)

Coho salmon run smaller, but 20-pounders aren't uncommon. (The world-record coho salmon – 33 pounds 4 ounces – was taken in New York in 1989.) Sockeye and pink salmon are smaller and less common.

BROOK TROUT

COHO SALMON

These open-water predators feed on schools of alewives and smelt that roam the cold depths, but will also feed near the surface. Coho salmon mature in 3 years before returning to the stream where they were stocked or hatched. Chinooks grow for an extra year before returning to their stream of origin, where they die after spawning.

Most salmon fishing requires a large, specially equipped boat for trolling the vast waters where these fish live. But during spawning runs, adult salmon move into tributary streams, and shorebound and wading fishermen can make great catches with spoons or large plugs.

White Bass

White bass are natives of the Great Lakes and the Mississippi River system, but they have been widely stocked beyond this range. This fish is a prolific breeder (one adult female may lay a half million eggs), a ravenous feeder and a tough fighter. All these attributes make white bass a favorite with anglers.

The white bass has silvery-white sides with dark stripes running from the gills back to the tail. Most white bass taken by anglers average around a pound in size. The world record, weighing 6 pounds 13 ounces, was caught in Virginia in 1989.

Early each spring, white bass make spawning runs up river and reservoir tributaries. (They lay and fertilize their eggs in pools below shallow riffles.) During this spawning run, white bass are particularly aggressive, and they can be caught in large numbers.

After they spawn, white bass move back into deep pools in rivers and open water in reservoirs.

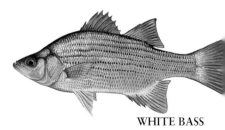

WHITE BASS

They gather in large schools, and they feed in a frenzy that sometimes leads them to strike anything that even vaguely resembles their prey. For this reason white bass are very popular wherever they are found. Fishing for white bass in the "jumps" (when they're surface feeding) is very productive and exciting!

Small shad are the white bass' main food source, though they'll also eat other minnows, crawfish and insects (particularly mayflies).

In table quality, white bass are delicious when taken from cool, clean waters. However, white bass caught from warm or silty waters tend to have a strong, musty flavor.

Stripers/Hybrids

"Striper" and "rockfish" are two nicknames for the saltwater striped bass. Native to the Atlantic Ocean and Gulf of Mexico, this fish can also live in freshwater, and it's been stocked extensively in rivers and large reservoirs throughout the mid- and western-United States. It does best where water temperature doesn't exceed 75° F, although it can live in warmer water. Most stripers caught in freshwater were raised in hatcheries and released as fingerlings, but natural reproduction does occur.

Stripers look like large white bass, except they are more elongated, and they grow huge in size. The world record (67 pounds 8 ounces) was caught in California in 1992.

Stripers are open-water fish, roving in schools through main-lake and river areas in search of prey. Because of their large size and tackle-busting ability, they are a favorite among thrill-seeking anglers. Stripers can be taken on both artificial lures (large jigs and minnow-like plugs) and live baitfish.

STRIPED BASS

"Hybrids" (also called "white rocks" and "wipers") are a cross between stripers and white bass. They do not occur naturally, but they are easy to raise in hatcheries. Since they are more tolerant of warm water than stripers, they are stocked heavily in southern and Midwestern reservoirs where earlier striper stockings failed. Hybrids look very much like stripers, except they are bulkier in shape, and the lines down their sides are often broken. Also, hybrids don't grow as large as stripers. The world-record striper (27 pounds 5 ounces) was caught in Arkansas in 1997.

Catfish

Catfish will never win a beauty contest, but they are beautiful, indeed, to millions of North American anglers. These whiskered fish live in warm-water rivers, ponds, lakes and reservoirs throughout much of the U. S. and southern Canada. Catfish are willing biters, and they're spirited fighters when hooked. They're also very good fried and served with French fries and hush puppies!

There are three common American catfish species: channel catfish, blue catfish and flathead catfish. All have a host of local nicknames.

Channel catfish have olive-blue sides fading to silver-white bellies. They also have small dark spots on their backs and sides. Channel cats live mostly in rivers or lakes with slow to moderate currents. They are the smallest of the three catfish species, rarely exceeding 25 pounds. The world record channel cat weighed 58 pounds even and was caught in South Carolina in 1964.

Blue catfish look very much like channels, except they don't have spots on their backs and sides.

FLATHEAD CATFISH

They grow larger than channel catfish. Blue cats occasionally exceed 100 pounds. The world record blue cat weighed 116 pounds 12 ounces and was caught in Arkansas in 2001. Blue catfish thrive in big, slow-moving rivers such as the Mississippi, Ohio, Tennessee and Missouri. They gang up in tailrace areas below dams on these rivers.

Flathead catfish are so-named because of their appearance. The flathead's mouth is long and flat, and its lower jaw is slightly longer than its upper jaw. Its back and sides are mottled brown tapering to a lighter belly. Flathead catfish live in a variety of waters, though they prefer current and clean water. The world-record flathead cat weighed 123 pounds and was caught in Kansas in 1998.

All three of these species share certain traits. They have a slick, scaleless skin. and feature eight barbels (whiskers) around the mouth. The barbels contain highly-developed smelling organs, which the fish use to sniff out and "taste" various foods. Catfish have one of the most highly developed senses of smell of all fish. Sometimes catfish rely more on their sense of smell to find food than their sense of sight.

Blue and channel catfish eat worms, insects, baitfish, crawfish, invertebrates, wild seeds, and a long list of other foods. Flathead cats, on the other hand, feed primarily on living foods – baitfish, crawfish, etc. Many catfish feed more at night than during the day. They feed mainly on the bottom, though they will move up and forage near the surface if a good feeding opportunity exists there.

Catfish spawn in late spring, after the water temperature reaches 70° F. Females lay eggs in holes in the bank, under logs, among rocks, or in other spots that offer some protection from current and concealment from predators.

Bullheads

Bullheads are members of the catfish family, and are often assumed to be small catfish. There is one easy way to tell them apart. Bullheads have rounded tails (Flatheads have rounded tails like bullheads, but are recognized by their long, flat mouth.)

There are three common species of bullheads in North America: black, brown and yellow. Their range covers most of the U. S. and southern Canada. They live in a variety of waters,

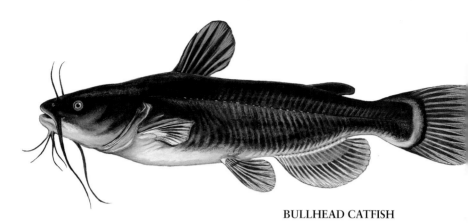

BULLHEAD CATFISH

from small ponds and marshes to large impoundments and rivers. Three other species (snail, spotted, and flat bullhead) are found in the Southeast. Bullheads prefer quiet, warm waters, and they usually hang close to bottom. They are highly tolerant of pollution and low oxygen content, which means they can survive in many waters where other species can't live.

Bullheads are usually much smaller than catfish. They rarely grow larger than 2 pounds. The world-record black bullhead weighed 8 pounds 15 ounces and was caught in New York in 1951. The world-record brown bullhead weighed 6 pounds 5 ounces and was caught in New York in 2002. The world-record yellow bullhead weighed 4 pounds 4 ounces and was caught in Arizona in 1984.

Bullheads share many of the same feeding and spawning habits as catfish. They're favorites of many panfish anglers, since they're plentiful and usually bite when other species won't.

CHAPTER 3

Where and How to Find Good Fishing Spots

My favorite way to fish is to paddle a canoe or wade along a free-running stream, casting a crawfish lure for smallmouth, spotted bass and other small sunfish. This type fishing is simple. It's very relaxing. The setting is usually beautiful, and stream fish typically bite with little hesitation. All these things combine for a wonderful outing.

Fish-filled streams are scattered throughout North America, and many receive virtually no fishing pressure. Anglers who become detectives can uncover these small flowing waters and enjoy great, unspoiled fishing on them.

Still, for reasons I don't understand, most anglers overlook streams and the light tackle methods I enjoy. Many are more attuned to big waters, fast boats and run-and-gun tactics. (I'm not complaining! The main reason streams offer good fishing is because they don't get much fishing pressure.)

Several years ago, I made a wonderful discovery – a stream full of fish almost untouched by other fishermen. A friend and I had received permission to hunt wild turkeys on a farm that was a two-hour drive from my home. Before hunting season we went there on a scouting trip and discovered that the farm had a beautiful creek flowing through it. I instantly knew that this stream had smallmouth bass "written all over it." It had clean water and was lined by gravel bars, rocky bluffs and hardwood trees whose branches spread over the water. There was a succession of shallow riffles and deep pools – perfect for harboring fish. Minnows seemed to linger near every rock and root wad.

When we returned to this area to go hunting, I also brought a spinning rod and my stream-fishing tackle box. We set up camp in a grassy pasture next to the creek. The next morning, after a few hours of chasing gobblers, I headed back to camp and rigged my rod to test the creek's potential. On the second cast I hooked a monster smallmouth! This fish engulfed my bait, jumped once, then headed downstream like a runaway train. I did my best to turn it, but it ran under a log and hung up. The next thing I knew, my 6-pound test line snapped, and the bass was gone.

I was stunned by this turn of events. I only got a quick glimpse, but I'm sure this smallmouth would

A father and son cast around flooded cypress trees in a state impoundment lake. Good public fishing waters abound throughout North America, and there are many different sources for locating them. These include state fish and wildlife agencies, tourism bureaus, city recreation departments, utility companies, public resource agencies, and military reservations.

have weighed at least 5 pounds. I waited a few seconds to regain my composure, then I set about casting again around the rocks and logs along the far side of the creek.

I caught several more smallmouth that afternoon, including a couple in the 3 pound class. I also landed at least a dozen rock bass and bluegill. This stream was jam-packed with fish, and they bit as though they'd never seen a lure.

Catfish and other fish species are plentiful in public waters throughout North America. A good way to find productive fishing waters is to speak with a biologist and asking his recommendation on spots to try.

This was one of my greatest fishing discoveries ever. I've been back numerous times since that day, and this stream has never disappointed me. Now when I go, I float all day in a canoe, covering around 6 miles of water. I concentrate only on the best spots – the holes below the riffles and the deeper runs with good cover and current. Over the years I've caught several smallmouth over 5 pounds, and a friend once landed a smallie that weighed close to 7 pounds.

Fishing spots this good are a rare find, but it's not difficult for beginning anglers to locate first-rate places where they can expect reasonable success, or better. The U. S. and Canada teem with good fishing holes, and many of them are open to the public. Besides streams, you can find fish in natural lakes, man-made reservoirs, swamps, rivers, farm ponds, beaver ponds, oxbow lakes, drainage canals, tailraces below dams, mining pits, city lakes, pay lakes, coastal marshes and other spots. Some of these places already get plenty fishing pressure but others, like my stream, await someone to discover them and enjoy their bounty.

As you learn more about fishing, you should also start looking for places where you can go fishing. Make a list of possibilities, and research them thoroughly to learn which ones are best. Doing this is a matter of knowing where to look, whom to ask and what information to collect. I guarantee, there is a broad range of fishing waters close to where you live, wherever you live!

Sometimes piers, catwalks and other bank structures are good places to fish. However, always secure permission before using a private pier or dock.

Following is a step-by-step guide for finding good fishing holes anywhere in North America.

Beginning the Search

Locating good fishing spots is like being a detective and unraveling a mystery. You collect information from many different sources, then you compare notes to see which spots are best. How good are they? How accessible are they? How much pressure do they get from other anglers?

Many agencies can provide information about public fishing spots. These include state fish and wildlife agencies, tourism bureaus, city recreation departments, utility companies, public resource agencies, and military reservations. Virtually all these agencies have web sites that list public fishing opportunities and contacts who can provide more details.

To start your search, log onto the web site www.recreation.gov. This site provides a state-by-state listing of all federal lands where public recreation – including fishing – is available. (Examples include federal reservoirs, national forests, national parks, national wildlife refuges, etc.) It also provides links to state agency web sites that will have their own wealth of information about fishing opportunities.

Another way to find fishing spots on-line is to go to a search engine (www.google.com) and type in "Fishing in _____ ," filling your state in the blank. You'll come up with thousands of leads.

Those who don't have Internet access can use the telephone and mail to obtain information. Call your state fish and wildlife agency, and ask for the public information office. Tell the person who answers that you're looking for places where you can go fishing. Check in your public library for a list of government agencies, then call them and ask for the public information or recreation branch.

When you're browsing web sites or talking to an information contact, try to obtain the following: (1) a list of public fishing spots near your home, and brochures, maps and other details about these spots; (2) the name, phone number and e-mail address of the biologist who manages these fisheries; (3) the names, phone numbers and e-mail addresses of fish/wildlife officers who patrol the spots on the list; and (4) any brochures listing fishing seasons, license requirements, creel limits and other pertinent regulations.

Sometimes biologists can provide detailed information about specific fisheries, orr, a biologist might know of another overlooked opportunity you can try. Don't be hesitant about calling a biologist who works for a public agency. Remember, he works for you! Also, biologists are usually eager to help people enjoy the benefits of their fisheries management efforts.

Many state fish and wildlife agencies maintain piers where the public can fish for free. Most of these have brush and other cover in the surrounding water to concentrate fish so anglers have a better chance of catching them.

Where and How to Find Good Fishing Spots 41

Federal- and state-managed lakes abound throughout North America, and many support plentiful fish populations. Anglers can locate such lakes in their area by consulting their local fish and wildlife agency.

The same is true for wildlife officers. These men and women spend much of their lives in the field, and they will probably know how good the fishing is in a lake/stream/pond in which you're interested. (Trout stocking locations, where hatchery-raised fish are released at publicized locations and times, are special fishing opportunities.)

Don't be shy about contacting these fish/wildlife professionals. They spend their lives working to provide the public with good fishing and hunting, and they enjoy helping license holders take advantage of it.

Bait and Tackle Shops, Other Info Sources

Virtually every community has a bait and tackle shop which can be an excellent source of information for finding good fishing. Bait shop operators talk to fishermen everyday, and they make it their business to keep up with what's biting, and where. Also, it's in their best interest to provide you with information to help you catch fish. By doing so, they're creating another customer. This is why you can usually trust the advice you get in a bait/tackle store.

Another helpful source is the outdoor writer at your local newspaper. Tell him you're a beginner looking for a good place to go fishing. Also, call your county agricultural extension service agent, and ask if he has any ideas. Do the same with the local boat/marine dealer. Ask him if he can provide names of fishing club members or local fishing experts who might help. In essence, contact anybody you can think of who has any connection to fishing. on where to go. You'll get plenty recommendations on where to go.

Don't overlook books, maps or pamphlets containing information about fishing in your area. Years ago a canoe enthusiast published a float guide for streams in the state where I live. I bought a copy, and it turned out to be a wealth of

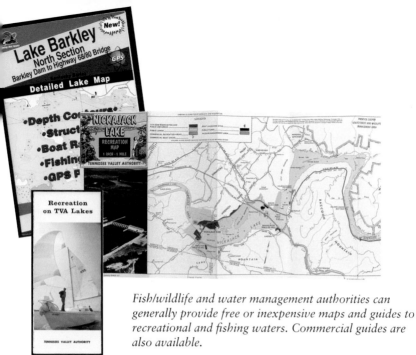

Fish/wildlife and water management authorities can generally provide free or inexpensive maps and guides to recreational and fishing waters. Commercial guides are also available.

information about access points, lengths of different floats, water depth and current, etc. It even rated fisheries in the various streams it covered. I've worn that book out studying it over the years. Similar books may be available in your area. Look for such printed material in libraries, bookstores and bait shops. Many bait shops sell maps of area lakes, fishing guidebooks and other helpful publications.

Fishing on Private Lands

While most of the advice above applies to public fishing waters, many excellent spots exist on private land. These include stock ponds, watershed lakes, irrigation ditches and reservoirs. Permission to fish private waters may not be easy to obtain, but there's no harm in asking. Some landowners will still allow fishing by those who ask in a direct, courteous manner.

Of course, such permission comes with the responsibility to show respect for the landowner and his property. Don't forget, you're his guest. Never litter his property. If a gate is closed, don't leave it open, if open, don't close it. Don't climb over wire fences and "ride them down." Don't drive off established roads or damage crops. Always offer to share what you

The only way to learn if a pond or small lake has good fishing is to test-fish it. Try a new spot at least three times before giving up on it. The first time you fish it, the fish might not be biting. Then, when you come back, you might make the catch of a lifetime!

catch. If you act responsibly and don't abuse your privilege, you will probably be welcomed to fish there again. But if you cause a problem, you'll be turned down the next time, and so will other fishermen who come after you.

Pay Lakes and Fishing Piers

One special opportunity for beginning anglers is pay lakes and fishing piers. These are commercial fishing establishments (catfish ponds, trout ponds, etc.) that are run for profit. At some places you pay a flat rate per hour of fishing. At others, you pay by the pound for fish you catch.

Pay lakes can be fun since they're heavily stocked and managed so anglers can catch plenty fish. They can also be expensive if you catch too many! When you sign in, make sure you know the rules and prices, then stay within your budget.

Rating Your Fishing Spots

After compiling a list of possible fishing spots, it's time to rate them. There are several criteria for doing so. How far away are they, and how difficult to reach? How much fishing pressure do they receive? If you don't have a boat, can you fish from the bank, bridge or pier? Is

Ethics & Etiquette

Play by the Rules Obey all fish and game laws. These are designed to protect fish and game populations and also to make sure that everybody has an equal chance to enjoy them.

A host of books, magazines and phamphlets are available featuring information about outdoor sports and fishing opportunities throughout the United States and Canada.

wade-fishing a possibility? If you have a boat, is a ramp or launch site available?

Next comes the fun part – test-fishing your top prospects to see how good they really are. I recommend test-fishing a new spot at least three times before writing it off. The first time, the fish might not be biting. But when you return, they might be actively feeding. If a particular lake, stream or pond is recommended by biologists, wildlife officers or other reputable sources, don't give up on it too soon.

Most of North America's large rivers and lakes offer good fishing for anglers who take the time to locate tham and learn their secrets.

Over the seasons, as you explore more and more, you will add to your list of fishing places, and you can upgrade continually. When you discover a good new spot, you can discard a marginal one. In a few seasons, you will have a repertoire of favorites where you can go and fish with confidence of catching something.

I still fish the smallmouth stream that I found so many years ago. I also routinely fish another stream, two big reservoirs, and a couple of farm ponds close to my house. I visit them as often as I can, and the more I fish them, the more I learn about their secrets. I still enjoy searching out and trying new spots, but day in and day out, I'll take the old proven places where memories flow with the currents, and the past and the future are joined in the next cast.

CHAPTER 4

Selecting Tackle

A long pole is a super-effective "fishing tool" for catching panfish. Most commercial poles (like the one illustrated above) have line holders and guides, while old-fashioned cane poles are rigged by tying a fixed length of line to the tip.

A basic fishing outfit has four components: a pole (or rod/reel), line, a terminal rig (hooks, sinkers, floats), and some type bait – live or artificial. Various combinations of these components can be used to catch any of the species described in Chapter 2. The trick, however, comes in selecting the right combination for the type and size fish you're targeting, with the fishing method and bait you plan to use.

Confusing? Visit a tackle or sporting goods store, and you'll find a huge variety of poles, rods, reels, lines, rigs, etc. Knowing what to buy and how to match different components can be intimidating. However, making good choices is easy if you understand the differences in these tackle items and the purposes for which they were designed. This chapter will explain these differences and provide information you need to make wise tackle selections. Then Chapter 6 will explain basic rigs and how to tie them, and Chapter 7 will cover baits.

A good way to think about tackle is "fishing tools." Various tackle items have specific purposes. You wouldn't choose a hammer to saw a board in two, and you shouldn't select a heavy bass outfit to go after bluegill or trout. Instead, you must learn to match the right "tool" to the "job" you wish to do. Anglers who do this will be much more effective – and have more fun – than others who pick the wrong "tools."

Component #1: The Pole or Rod

When I was growing up, I'd go fishing with my dad, and he would cut wild cane off the riverbank and rig them for our poles. They worked very well on the panfish we sought.

However, over the years I became more sophisticated in my tackle needs and fishing techniques. Today my tackle closet holds numerous casting, spinning and fly rods in a variety of actions and lengths. Again, these are "tools" for different types of fishing methods. Veteran anglers usually own several outfits that match a range of species and techniques for catching them.

Still, a beginner should start with one multipurpose fishing rod/ reel combo that can be used for several situations. As you get more involved in fishing, you'll probably want more specialized tackle. But when you're getting started, you don't have to – and shouldn't – spend a small fortune on tackle. Your first outfit can be simple and inexpensive, yet versatile enough to catch many different species of fish.

Spinning tackle is great for casting small lures/ baits for panfish. A spinning reel mounts beneath the rod on a straight handle. These reels have an exposed spool and a revolving "bail" that spins around as the handle is turned, thereby wrapping line around the spool.

Differences Between Poles and Rods

Mechanically speaking, a fishing pole or rod is a lever that serves as an extension of the fisherman's arm. With either, you get more length and leverage for presenting a bait, setting the hook, and battling and landing a fish once it's hooked.

Poles are longer than rods. The line is fixed to the end of a pole, and the bait is presented by swinging the line out. Poles aren't meant for casting. Conversely, rods are shorter than poles, and a rod is normally fitted with a reel that holds line for casting a bait out away from the angler.

Therefore, how you fish determines whether you need a pole or a rod. If you're going after bluegill or crappie close to the bank or shoreline, a pole may be the best choice. But if you're trying for bass away from shore, or if you're fishing in deep water for catfish or walleye, you need a rod and reel so you can get extra casting distance or depth.

Rods/reels are far more versatile than poles because of their "reach." They can be used in many more fishing situations. Also, rods may substitute for poles in some close-in fishing situations. This is

This travel spinning rod seperates into several short sections for easy packing.

why today, probably 90% of all fishing is done with rods/reels.

Poles

Poles come in three main materials: natural cane, fiberglass and graphite. They are sold in various lengths, typically from 8 feet to 16 feet – or longer! Some poles are stiff and strong (heavy action) for catfish and other large fish. Other poles are limber (light action) for catching crappie, bluegill and other small panfish.

Cane poles are simplest and least expensive: around $5. However, fiberglass and graphite poles are more durable and sensitive to delicate bites, and they offer more features. Many fiberglass or graphite poles are collapsible, making them easy to transport. These poles may cost $15 for the simplest fiberglass model to close to $100 for a sensitive graphite collapsible pole.

Some poles come with a line holder, which allows an angler to change the length of line he's using – let some out or take some up. One type line holder is a simple reel that mounts on the pole's butt. Another type is a metal bracket around which excess line is wrapped. A pole with a line holder usually has guides like a casting rod, or the line is run through the middle of

a hollow pole and out a hole in the tip. In either case, the reel or line holder on a pole is meant simply for adjusting line length, not casting.

Rods

Buying a rod is more complicated than buying a pole, since there are many more factors to consider. Rods come in different designs (casting, spinning), materials, lengths, actions, and handle and guide components. They are sold in a broad range of prices, from inexpensive to very expensive. All these variables can confound a fisherman shopping for his first outfit.

However, there is one simple way to avoid making a bad decision: seek the advice of an experienced angler. Find someone to help you make a good choice. This may be the salesman in an outdoor store or tackle department. Tell

Shown below from top to bottom: A pistol-grip casting rod, a standard- grip casting rod and a fly rod.

him what type fishing you want to do – species, methods, locations (if you know them), and he should be able to outfit you. If he can't, find someone who can.

Rod Features

Following are brief looks at the different features of fishing rods. Having a basic understanding of them will help you select the rod that best suits your needs.

ROD TYPE – Rods are designed to match different types of reels. There are four basic types of reels: baitcasting, spinning, spin-cast, and fly. Casting rods are designed for use with baitcasting or spincast reels. Spinning rods are used with spinning reels, and fly-rods are designed for use with flyreels. Each type rod has its special uses and advantages/ disadvantages.

Deciding whether you need a casting, spinning or fly-fishing outfit is the first decision when buying tackle. The next section in this chapter explains the different types of rod/reel combinations and the fishing methods to which each is best-suited.

LENGTH – Most fishing rods measure 5-7 feet long, though highly specialized rods may be shorter or longer. Long rods offer more leverage. They can generally cast farther, but they are harder to cast accurately. Also, they may be awkward to use, especially for beginners. Short rods offer less leverage

Spinning and bait-casting rods are available with a wide range of handle styles and materials.

and casting distance, but they are more accurate for close-in casting. Best overall rod lengths for general fishing purposes are 5 1/2 -6 1/2 feet.

ACTION – "Action" refers to a rod's stiffness (strength) and how this stiffness is built into the design of the rod. A rod's action has a direct effect on the size baits a rod can cast effectively and the size fish it can handle. Standard rod actions are: ultralight, light, medium-light, medium, mediumheavy and heavy. A rod's action is usually printed on the rod just above the handle. (This printed material also lists recommended line sizes and lure weights for the rod.)

Ultralight rods are very limber. They are best for casting little baits (for example, 1/32 oz.) for bluegill, trout, perch and other small fish. Heavy-action rods are extremely stiff and powerful. They are best for casting heavy baits (1/2-1 ounce-plus) and catching such fish as trophy bass, stripers and big catfish. The stiffer the rod (i.e., the "heavier its action"), the more difficult it is to cast light, small baits. On the other hand, the lighter a rod's action, the less well-suited it is for casting heavy baits. It is crucial to match rod action, line size and bait size for maximum performance.

MID-WEIGHT RODS – light, medium-light and medium – are the most versatile and usually the best choice for beginning fishermen. With a 6-foot medium- light rod, you can land everything from bass and catfish to walleye, white bass, crappie, pike and other species. You need a heavy-action rod only when going after muskies, trophy pike, stripers or the biggest bass in the thickest cover.

ONE-PIECE/MULTI-PIECE – Most rods are constructed in one long piece. However, other rods are made in two or more pieces that can be joined. Onepiece rods are stronger and more sensitive, though multi-piece rods provide adequate strength and sensitivity for most fishing situations. The main advantage of a multi-piece rod is convenience in storing and carrying. It can be "broken down" and kept on a closet shelf or transported in a car's trunk.

MATERIALS – Most modern fishing rods are made from fiberglass, graphite, or a combination of these two materials. Fiberglass rods are flexible yet durable. They are also less expensive than graphite rods. Their drawback is that fiberglass rods weigh more. Also, fiberglass rods are less sensitive to light bites than graphite

Spin-cast reels are also called "push-button" reels. These reels have a closed hood over the line spool, and line plays out through a hole in the center of the hood.

rods. Conversely, graphite rods are lighter and more sensitive. Their drawbacks are higher cost and brittleness. A graphite rod that is mishandled will break easily.

When buying a graphite rod, you get what you pay for. Graphite rods run from a around $20 to over $100. What's the difference? Some graphite material is stronger, lighter weight and more sensitive to touch than others. High-end rods are extremely light, strong and sensitive, and their higher cost reflects these qualities.

Perhaps the best value in a beginning outfit is a low to mid-priced graphite rod or a good quality fiberglass rod. Either of these rods will offer great service at a reasonable price.

HANDLES – Rod handles come in a range of designs and materials.

This is mostly a matter of preference – what feels best to the user. Some anglers like straight handles; others prefer a pistol-grip handle. Many rods have long handles (a foot or more) that facilitate two-hand casting and extra support (hook it under your armpit) when fighting a big fish. Materials vary from cork (the best in my opinion) to plastic or foam.

My advice is: if it feels okay, it is okay. If a rod handle seems comfortable in the tackle store, it will be likewise on the water.

Casting, Spinning or Fly Tackle

When shopping for a new outfit, should you choose casting, spinning or fly tackle? Again, this depends on how you plan to fish (bait size, line size, etc.) and the type and size fish you will target.

ROUND BAIT CASTING

FLY

SPINNING

SPIN-CAST

LOW PROFILE BAIT CASTING

Let's start with casting tackle. Again, casting rods match up with baitcasting and spin-cast reels. These reels mount in the reel seat on top of the rod in front of the handle.

Baitcasting reels are also called "open face reels" and "revolving spool reels." When a bait is cast out, its weight pulls line off a baitcasting reel's exposed spool. Thumb pressure on the open spool is used to slow the bait and stop the cast at the desired distance.

Spin-cast reels, also called "push-button reels," have a spool that is enclosed inside a hood that covers the front of the reel. Line plays out through a small hole in front of the hood. To make a cast, an angler pushes and holds the thumb button down. He makes his backcast, then releases the button during the forward cast. When the button is released, the line plays out smoothly, then the user pushes the thumb button again to stop the cast.

Casting rods and these two reel types are normally stronger than spinning reels, and they are used with heavier line and baits to fish for bigger fish. Also, baitcasting outfits are the most accurate type of casting tackle. With practice, baitcasters can become very precise in casting distance by using direct thumb pressure on the reel spool to control casting speed and arc.

Spinning reels hang under the rod on a straight handle. These reels have an exposed spool and a revolving "bail" that spins around as the handle is turned, thereby wrapping line around the spool. For casting, the angler catches and holds the line on his forefinger, the bail is tripped out of the way, and the line is released during the forward portion of the cast. The line coils off the spool with almost no resistance. This allows anglers to use spinning tackle to cast very small baits or lures.

Spinning tackle is routinely used by anglers who go after smaller panfish such as bluegill, small bass, crappie, trout, walleye, etc. Also, larger spinning outfits can be used interchangeably with casting tackle to fish for bigger fish.

Fly-rods/reels are the epitome of specialty fishing. Fly-fishing tackle is used to cast small dry flies, artificial nymphs, streamers (wet flies), popping bugs and other baits that imitate insects, small larvae, etc. These flies and bugs weigh next to nothing, so it's impossible to cast them with casting or spinning tackle. In fact, in fly-casting, the angler uses the weight of the

Baitcasting reels are used for bigger lures/baits and heavy-duty fishing. When a bait is cast out, its weight pulls line off a baitcasting reel's exposed spool. The angler applies thumb pressure on the open spool to slow the bait and stop the cast at the desired distance.

line (instead of the lure) to achieve casting distance. He "false casts" (whips the rod back and forth over his shoulder) while letting out more line through the rod's guides. When he has enough line out to reach his target, he completes his cast by driving forward with the rod and allowing the line to settle to the water. The fly or bug just happens to be tagging along on the end of the line on a clear, thin "tippet."

Fly-fishing will frequently take fish when casting and spinning techniques are doomed to failure. This is because fly-fishing allows anglers to "match the hatch" when fish are feeding on tiny insects and larvae. However, fly-fishing is difficult to learn, and beginning anglers should master the basics of casting and spinning before they progress into fly-fishing.

Fishing Line

Fishing line is the actual link between angler and fish, so it's not something to take lightly. Anglers must choose the right line for their particular tackle and method, and they must know how to care for their line so it will last longer.

There are two basic types of lines available to anglers:

monofilament and "superlines." Monofilament is the most widely used. This extruded nylon line is a good choice for many different situations. It comes in a wide range of break strengths, called "pound test." (For instance, 6 pound test line will break when put under 6 pounds of pressure.) Monofilament lines have some stretch. They are very sensitive in terms of feel. They are abrasion resistant. They are also relatively inexpensive. One hint: don't scrimp when buying monofilament line. Buy premium quality line, not the bargain basement variety. An extra dollar or two spent on premium monofilament line is a good investment for successful fishing!

Superlines are a braid of many thin gel-spun polyethylene fibers. Some superlines are "fused" (the braided fibers are welded together). Other superlines are "non-fused," but they all have similar qualities. Superlines are much stronger than equivalent diameter sizes in monofilament. For instance, ten-pound superline is roughly the same diameter as 4-pound monofilament. Superlines have almost no stretch. They are very limp and extremely sensitive in feel. Their smaller diameter allows for longer

A rod/reel/line combination should be "balanced" to provide maximum performance. This means that a light action rod should be matched with a light action reel and small line to cast smaller lures/baits. Conversely, a heavy action rod should be mated with a heavy reel and line.

casts. Diving baits run deeper on superline than on monofilament.

Superlines' main drawback is their cost – significantly higher than monofilament. Most beginning anglers start out fishing with monofilament because it's less expensive and easier to handle.

Monofilament line comes in a variety of colors. Clear, green and fluorescent blue are the most popular shades. A good rule of thumb is to match line color to water color: clear line in clear water; green in

slightly stained water; and fluorescent blue in dingy water. Also, fluorescent blue is a good choice when anglers need to watch their line to detect subtle bites. Slight twitches that signal bites are much easier to spot in fluorescent blue line than in clear or green.

Many fishing experts swear that fish are scared by line that is too visible. Others believe that line visibility doesn't make any difference. (Some anglers use bright yellow or orange line in clear water, and they still catch fish!) Nobody knows who's right, but I don't take a chance. Unless I'm using a technique where I need to watch for line movement, I follow the recommendations given above.

Which size line is best? Several factors go into this answer. First, tackle must be "balanced" (see next section). You should use light line with light tackle and heavier line with heavy tackle. Again, most rods list recommended line sizes in the "fine print" above the handle.

As a general rule, 4-8 lb. test line is best for panfish like bluegill, crappie and walleye. For average-size bass, catfish, pike and similar-sized species, use 8- 12 lb. test. For the biggest of these species, or when fishing in heavy weeds or snags, 15-25 lb. test line might be appropriate.

Many beginning anglers buy combo outfits where the rod, reel and line come packaged together. Then the line choice decision is already made for you. Most combo outfits come with line that is in the 8-12 lb. test range.

The Concept of Balanced Tackle

One of the most important things to remember in buying tackle is to "balance" all the components of your outfit. Balanced tackle casts and retrieves lures/baits better and plays fish more efficiently than tackle that is unbalanced.

Some reels are large, sturdy and a good match for a heavyaction rod. Other reels are small and light, and these should be mated with light action rods. This is true with baitcasting, spin-cast and spinning tackle. Remember to match heavy with heavy and light with light.

The same concept applies to line. Heavy-action outfits work best with line that's 15 lb. test or heavier. Medium-action tackle matches well with line in the 10- 15 lb. test range. Light-action tackle should be spooled with 4- 8 lb. test. Ultra-light tackle works best with 2-6 lb. test line. (These line weights pertain to monofilament line. If a superline is preferred, select a line with a diameter that corresponds to the appropriate pound test size. In other words, 30 lb. test superline may have the same diameter as 12 lb. test monofilament. This information is normally given on the line package.)

The final component in balancing tackle is the lure or bait. It's impractical to cast a 1/16 oz. lure on an ultra-light outfit spooled with 4 lb. test monofilament. Conversely, it's impossible to cast a 1/16 oz. lure on heavy-action tackle. The lure isn't heavy enough to pull line off the reel. Use light-action tackle to cast lightweight lures (up to 1/8 oz.), and heavy-action tackle to cast heavy lures (1/2 oz. or heavier). There is some room for

Monofilament fishing line is offered in various colors and proprietary polymer formulas. Monofilament lines are both flexible and strong.

overlap in the intermediate tackle actions and lure weights.

Again, the best advice is to seek the advice of an experienced salesman or fishing friend. This should insure making good tackle choices. If your tackle isn't balanced, you will be handicapped from the start!

Adding Line Onto a Reel

Spooling line onto a reel must be done correctly. Improper spooling can lead to backlashes, line twist, loss of casting distance and other nuisances.

To spool line onto a baitcasting reel, run the line through the tip guide, then through all rod guides to the reel. Run the line through the reel's level wind (small guide which feeds line on/off the reel). Loop the line around the reel spool and tie it on with a line end knot (see Chapter 6). Snug the line tightly to the spool, and use clippers to clip the tag end close to the knot. Then have a friend hold the line in front of the rod tip, and run a pencil through the spool so it will rotate freely as the line comes off the spool. Use the reel handle to crank line onto the reel. Hold the rodtip up and keep slight pressure on the line so it goes on the reel spool uniformly. Add line to

Braiding technology and improved extrusion techniques have allowed the introduction of "superlines" that are both thinner and stronger than monofilament.

within a quarter inch of the top of the spool or to the level indicated in the reel instructions.

With a spin-cast reel, again run the line through the rod guides down to the reel. Unscrew the reel hood, poke the line through the hole in the center of the hood, tie it around the reel spool with a line end knot, and replace the hood. Then reel on line until it is an eighthinch from the outside edge of the spool. (You will have to unscrew the hood to check how much line you've added.)

With a spinning reel, run the line through the rod guides down to the reel. Open the bail (flip it down),

License and Limit Always buy required fishing licenses. Funds from license sales go back to maintain and improve fishing. Learn the creel and length limits where you fish. Never take more fish or smaller fish than you're supposed to.

Using fresh, good quality line is an important key to angling success. When you're fighting a fish is no time to worry about your line breaking.

tie the line around the reel spool with a line end knot, and close the bail (flip it back up). Next, lay the filler spool on the floor so line will coil off in the same direction the reel spool turns when you crank the handle. With a right-hand reel, the spool will turn clockwise, so lay the filler spool on the side that allows line to come off clockwise. This prevents line twist. Add line to within a quarter-inch of the edge of the reel spool or to the level indicated in the reel instructions.

Tying Line Onto a Pole

Poles are easy to rig with line. If a pole has a reel or line keeper, simply pull out line and run it through the guides or center of the pole and out the tip. Adjust the line length as desired.

If the pole doesn't have a reel or line keeper, tie the line onto the pole 18 inches down from the tip. Then wrap line around the pole candy-cane style to the tip, and tie it again. This wrapping provides extra support and strength to the pole tip. Then adjust the line to whatever length line is desired, and clip it off. Usually, the line should be approximately the same length as the pole, or slightly shorter.

Taking Care of Fishing Line

It's important to maintain fishing line in the best possible condition so it will keep its strength and provide top service.

Monofilament is very hardy and dependable, but excessive heat and direct sunlight will weaken it. Don't leave line in sunlight for long time periods when it's not being used. This is true for line on reels and for filler spools.

Avoid storing monofilament in a hot garage, attic or boat locker. The ideal place to store your fishing rods/reels and filler spools is in a cool room or closet.

Don't allow your line to come in contact with gasoline, oil, sunscreen or other chemical products. Some products won't have any effect on monofilament line, but others will weaken it or cause it to become brittle. Don't take a chance!

Monofilament that sits unused on a reel for a long time can develop "memory," which causes the line to come off in coils or loops like a slinky. This cuts down on casting distance and sensitivity. To solve this problem, remove the line spool from the reel before going fishing and soak it a few hours in a bowl of water. Water will actually penetrate the nylon-based monofilament and soften it, eliminating the coils.

Even with the best of care, monofilament line will age, and it's a good idea to replace it periodically. Two line changes a year will be sufficient for most anglers – at the beginning and middle of the fishing season. New line is cheap insurance against breakage when you're fighting a trophy fish!

Last, it's important to check monofilament line for nicks and

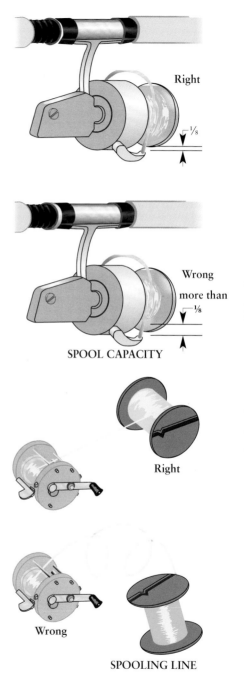

Right

Wrong
more than ⅛

SPOOL CAPACITY

Right

Wrong

SPOOLING LINE

abrasions close to the bait or lure. "Mono" can become battle- damaged when playing a fish or when rubbing against rocks, brush, etc. Check your line every few minutes by running it between your thumb and forefinger. If you feel a rough spot, cut your bait off, clip the line off above the rough spot, then retie the bait. It's much better to sacrifice a couple of feet of line than to suffer a break-off when you're fighting a big fish.

Superline is hardier than monofilament, and it doesn't need the attention that the latter does. Still, here are three tips for keeping superline in the best possible shape. One, keep it out of direct sunlight, which can fade superline's color. Two, if fishing in muddy or algae-filled water, rinse superline with clear water after use. Superline that's not rinsed will develop a bad odor from bacteria trapped inside the braided line. And three, if fraying is evident, clip off the frayed section and retie. Superline won't weaken like monofilament, but bad frays should still be eliminated.

Summary on Rods, Reels, Line

As stated earlier, as a beginning angler you should start out with one or two outfits. As you gain experience, you may add other rod/reel combos to match special fishing methods you will learn. But at first, you should purchase a middle-of-the-road outfit that's suitable for a range of fish species and techniques.

Here is my recommendation: start with a 6-foot medium action rod made from fiberglass or graphite. Match this with a spin-cast reel spooled with 10 lb. test monofilament. A good quality rod/reel in a combo pack will cost $25-50.

Then, if you can afford a second outfit, buy a 6-foot light action spinning rod/reel with 6 or 8 lb. test monofilament line. This outfit will cost approximately the same price. With these two outfits, you will be equipped to go after everything from medium-sized gamefish to the smallest bluegill and perch.

As you progress in this sport, you will increase your skill and develop a need for more specialized tackle. But when starting out, it's best to keep your fishing tools simple (and inexpensive!). You can't run before you walk, and you don't need sophisticated tackle until you master the basics.

CHAPTER 5

Accessories for Fishing

Fishing is gadget-oriented! If you don't believe this, walk through a tackle store or sporting goods department and check out the products available. Beyond rods, reels, line and lures, there is a broad array of accessories designed to make fishing more efficient and con-

A fisherman's tool is a musthave for anglers. Such a tool will be used frequently to tune lures, pry hooks from fish, change hooks on a lure, and handle other chores. Some tools include a hook sharpener, knife blade, screwdriver and other useful accessories.

venient. But as the old saying goes, some are designed to catch fish, while others are designed to catch fishermen. Fishing gadgets will truly range from the practical to the outlandish!

Beyond a pair of basic rod/reel outfits and bait or lures, beginners need a small collection of other items to participate in this sport. Fortunately, this "must-have" list is small and relatively inexpensive – probably no more than $50 total.

Then there are many other accessories that are handy, but not essential. If you'd like to own them and can afford them, fine. They will likely add extra pleasure to your fishing.

And finally, there are the gimmicks that should be avoided. These are made and marketed to prey on beginners' lack of experience. These products usually come with unrealistic promises of success. Remember, nothing in fishing is guaranteed. If a product sounds too good to be true, it probably is. Save your money, and depend on using basic knowledge and practical products to catch fish.

Following are two lists. The first includes accessories that you should definitely purchase when getting into fishing. These are items that you will take and use on each outing. The second list includes fishing accessories that are non-essential but which are practical and handy to have. These items can be purchased as your needs dictate and your finances allow.

Must-Have Fishing Accessories

TACKLE BOX/BAG – Every fisherman must have a tackle box or bag for toting tackle and gear. In essence, this is like a portable

Besides basic tackle, anglers need a small collection of accessories to participate in this sport. On the list of necessities are a tackle box, line clippers, needlenose pliers, polarized sunglasses and sunscreen. Non-essential-but-handy extras include a fishing very, and for stream anglers, wading shoes.

locker. It will carry such necessities as bait/lures, extra line, terminal tackle (hooks, sinkers, floats, swivels, etc.), and other small items.

I've actually fished with anglers who carried their tackle in small duffle bags, or even in paper bags. What a mess, especially when the paper bags got wet! To find something, these fishermen would have to stir around looking for it. This is why a hard plastic tackle box or soft-sided tackle packer is a good investment. They have compartments and storage boxes to keep tackle organized and accessible for quick location and use.

I recommend a medium-sized box (not one that's too large)!

A sharp, thin-bladed fillet knife is useful when the time comes for cleaning and processing your catch.

Select a box or packer that allows you to arrange compartments to suit your specific needs. Also, make sure your tackle box has a deep, roomy area to hold spare line, pliers, sunscreen and other extras.

Every angler needs a tackle box or some type of storage system to tote his lures and accessories and to keep them organized.

A rainsuit isn't on the "must-have" list, but it's a very handy accessory for warding off rain and spray. Even wearing a rainsuit that's much too big is better than not having one when the sky opens up.

As your involvement in fishing grows, you can continue adding tackle and lure boxes and arranging them for specific needs and/or species. My personal tackle packer is a soft-sided (cloth) system with individual plastic boxes, and I mix and match according to what type fishing I plan to do. I have several boxes of bass lures and tackle, one box with small jigs for panfish, another box of hooks, sinkers and floats, another box with stream-fishing lures, another with catfish paraphernalia, etc. Then, when I'm going fishing, I choose the tackle box that I need for that day.

FISHERMAN'S TOOL – This is a fancy name for needle-nose pliers. Some fisherman's tools also have a hook sharpener, line/wire cutter and other built-in features. The most frequent use of a fisherman's tool is prying hooks from fish, especially those that are embedded in the gullet. The needle-noses can reach deep into a fish's mouth and remove a hook safely and with minimal damage. Also, a fisherman's tool is handy for tuning lures (see section on artificial lures), adding or removing a hook from a split ring and other tasks. The best fish-erman's tools come with a handy belt holder.

LINE CLIPPERS – This is an angler's term for fingernail clippers that are used for cutting line. Buy line clippers with a lanyard for hanging the clippers around your neck. This keeps the clippers convenient for quick, easy use when changing lures, retying a frayed knot, etc.

FISHING CAP – Fishermen need a good cap to block the sun off their face and shade their eyes. Shading helps anglers see underwater to spot rocks, logs and fish. For hot weather, wear a mesh cap that's a light color – white or tan. In cold weather, you'll need something warmer. Also, for stream or pond fishing, a camo cap is a good choice.

POLARIZED SUNGLASSES – Sunglasses cut down on glare off the water, and polarized sunglasses actually allow you to see beneath the surface. They make it even easier to spot underwater objects that fish hang around, or to see fish themselves. Also, sunglasses protect eyes from flying objects, especially hooks. Keep sunglasses attached by a lanyard around your neck to keep from losing them when leaning over the water.

FISHERMAN'S TOWEL – This is a convenience item, but it's very nice to have when handling fish or messy live bait. Having a towel keeps your pant legs from getting dirty. Consider purchasing a towel with a belt clip to keep it handy at all times.

SUNSCREEN – Having and using sunscreen is absolutely essential for fishermen. People who are in the sun a lot are at risk from skin cancer, which can be deadly. Before going fishing, apply sunscreen to all exposed skin (arms, hands, face, neck, ears, etc.) Use sunscreen that's at least 15 SPF, and higher is better.

FISH STRINGER – If you will be fishing from the bank or from a boat that doesn't have a live well, you will need a fish stringer to keep your catch. Stringers come in two types: rope stringer, and chain stringer. A rope stringer has a metal point on the end. The point is guided through a fish's gill plate and out the mouth, and individual fish slide down the cord on top of each other. A chain stringer has individual safetypin snaps for holding fish. A chain stringer is better for keeping fish alive. Neither type stringer is very expensive.

Nonessential but Recommended Accessories

PFD (PERSONAL FLOTATION DEVICE) – Not many anglers wear a PFD when fishing off a bank, pier or bridge, but it's still a good idea, especially if you're not a strong swimmer. Also, a Coast Guard-certified PFD is required by law when fishing from a boat. (Always wear your life preserver when the boat is running. You don't have to wear it when the boat is not in operation, but it must always be in your possession.) One comfortable, convenient style PFD is the foam vest. Also, a new inflatable CO_2 type vest is extremely handy. It's so compact, you forget you have it on. But if you need it, you simply pull the lanyard, and the vest inflates instantly.

RAINSUIT – A rainsuit is obviously good for keeping you dry in a rainstorm. It's also good for shielding against spray when riding in a boat. The best rainsuits are made from waterproof, breathable fabric like Gore-Tex, but these are expensive. For starters, consider an inexpensive polyvinyl suit that comes in a small carry pouch.

FISHING VEST/TACKLE BELT – A vest or tackle belt is extremely handy for fishing streams or ponds where you will walk a lot. You wear your tackle instead of carrying it! You can store lures, tackle and accessories in pockets or compartments. Keep your vest or belt stocked, and you'll have everything ready when it's time to go fishing.

TOTE BAG – A tote or duffle bag is handy for carrying fishing accessories that won't fit into a tackle box. Any small bag with carry straps will do. By keeping all these accessories

Fishermen using live bait need some way to keep their bait fresh and handy. A minnow bucket, cricket cage or worm box works for most, but anglers can go fancier, like this aerated cooler for holding goldfish for catfishing.

packed in one bag, you're not as likely to forget something.

LIVE BAIT CONTAINER – If you fish with live bait, you'll need a minnow bucket, worm box, cricket cage or some other container to keep your bait alive and healthy.

CAMERA – If you practice catch-and-release, a camera is handy for photographing trophy fish before you let them go. This way you can prove your big fish stories. A digital camera is best, since you can download images and email them to friends.

REEL REPAIR KIT – A small reel repair kit can be a lifesaver for inthe- field repairs or adjustments. I carry a kit that includes small screwdrivers (flathead and Phillips), an adjustable wrench, and a container of reel oil. I use my kit several times a year to work on reels and to handle other small maintenance chores.

LURE RETRIEVER – If you fish from a boat, a lure retriever can save a lot of money in lost lures. If you hang your lure on an underwater object, you can position the boat directly over the lure and use a retriever to free it. Lure retrievers come in two types: a heavy weight on a string, and a collapsible pole. The pole works better, but it's bulkier and more costly. A weight/string can be kept in a tackle box or tote bag. With either type, it only takes a few lures saved to recover the cost of the retriever.

This fisherman's tool includes needle-nose pliers, line cutters, knife blade, and multiple accessories ranging from bottle openers to screwdrivers.

If It Sounds Too Good, It Probably Is...

Every year I see advertisements for fishing products that sound too good to be true. They make outlandish claims of success. "Buy this product, and load the boat. Fish can't resist it!"

Keep your money in your pocket. As I said earlier, if a fishing lure or accessory sounds too good, it probably is. The secret to successful fishing is not buying and

trying every new gimmick that hits the market. Instead, the secret to successful fishing is understanding fish habits and using a logical strategy to catch them.

This isn't to say that all new fishing products are hoaxes; far from it! Many new products have legitimate value in terms of making fishing easier and more successful. (When the depthfinder first appeared, many anglers were doubtful about this "electronic wonder," but it changed fishing forever.)

Still, don't buy new gadgets on impulse and expect them to produce instant results. If a new product is legitimate, it'll be around

Every angler needs a good fishing hat or cap. Many veterans prefer a hat that shades the ears and back of the neck.

for a long time. Wait until the jury – more experienced anglers – returns a verdict. Watch for product reviews in fishing magazines and on TV shows. In some cases you can buy knowledge (via books, videos, magazines), but you can't buy experience. It takes both these things to become a successful fisherman.

Basic Fishing Rigs

Using the right rig is crucial in fishing. A rig is whatever you tie onto your line to hold and present your bait or lure to the fish. Anglers who know how to match and adjust rigs to particular fishing situations will get more action than those who don't.

Several years back I went fishing below a dam on a local river for sauger and white bass, and while I was there I learned a lesson that's stuck with me ever since.

Fish were feeding in the swift current, where water was being released through the dam. I anchored in a slack area and proceeded to cast a diving crankbait across the current, retrieving it back in a looping track downstream. Every couple of dozen casts I'd get a bite and reel in another fish. I thought I was doing pretty well.

But then I started watching another angler in a boat anchored several yards up from me. He was obviously using a different technique, casting directly toward the face of the dam. Then he reeled in slowly, holding his rod up as his bait worked back with the current. And he was getting a fish at almost every cast! It seemed as if his rod was constantly bowed over from fighting another large sauger or white bass.

After a couple of hours, he began stowing his gear to leave. I pulled up my anchor, idled over beside his boat and commented, "I couldn't help but notice how many fish you've been catching. Would you mind sharing your secret?"

He was willing to help. "It's no secret," he said. "I'm using small shad minnows, the type the fish are feeding on. I use a bottom-bumping rig to work the minnows down-current, the way the bait naturally moves. This rig keeps my bait close to the bottom without hanging up, and I'm casting into breaks between the seams of fast water. This is where most of the feeding is going on. The fish don't have to work so hard to hang there, and the adjacent currents wash the minnows to them."

So, he did have secrets, three of them! One was his bait. The second was his rig, and the third was his method of using it. His presentation was much more natural and effective than mine, and he'd loaded his boat with fish. Even if you're in the right spot, you can still fare poorly if you're not using the right bait, rig and technique.

Components of a Fishing Rig

A fishing rig is whatever you tie on the end of your line to hold and present your bait. It's a combination of hooks, sinkers, floats, snaps, swivels, leaders and the knots that tie everything together.

Fishermen use many different rigs for special fishing situations. There are rigs for live bait and artificial lures. There are rigs for fishing on bottom, on the surface, and in between. There are rigs for trolling, drifting, staying in one spot. There are rigs for fishing in current and still water. There are rigs for using more than one bait at a time. This list could go on and on. Beginners don't need to learn a lot of complicated rigs, for now, a few basic rigs will provide the means for catching most popular species in a wide variety of settings.

Fishing Knots: Holding the Rig Together

One thing all fishing rigs have in common is knots, so learning to tie knots is the logical starting point in a discussion of rigs. You will have to tie knots several times on each fishing trip, so learn this lesson well!

Tying a knot in a fishing line weakens it. An improperly tied knot can reduce line strength by more than 50%. But a knot that's properly tied will retain up to 95% of the full strength of the line.

Using the right style and size hook is an important part of fishing success. Match size of the hook to the size fish you're after. For instance, with little fish like trout, sunfish and yellow perch, smaller hooks are better.

Strong knots that won't slip or break will produce more fish.

Following are instructions for tying six fundamental knots. The first three are my picks for tying line to hooks, sinkers, swivels, etc. The fourth knot is used to tie a loop in the line. The fifth knot is the one I use to tie two lines together when I'm adding line to my reel. And the sixth is a good knot for adding line to an empty reel spool.

When tying any of these knots, I always follow two rules: before snugging a knot tight, I always spit on it to lubricate it. This saliva reduces line-weakening friction and heat buildup as the knot draws tight. And I always leave 1/8 inch of line when I clip the tag end. This allows for some slippage in the knot without it coming undone.

TRILENE KNOT – This is the knot I use for 90% of my fishing.

I tie it almost every time I need a line-to-hook or line-to-lure connection. It's a very strong knot, and it takes only a small amount of practice to master. I highly recommend it.

To tie the Trilene knot, run approximately 4 inches of line through the hook eye, loop it around and pass it through the hook eye again. Pull the line to

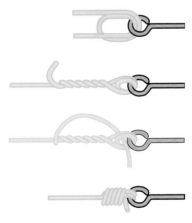

TRILENE KNOT

draw the loop down to a small diameter (1/4-1/2 inch). Now catch and hold this loop between your thumb and forefinger to keep it open. Wrap the end of the line around the standing line 5 times. Last, pass the end back through the loop, and snug the knot tight by pulling the standing line and the hook in opposite directions. Trim the tag end.

PALOMAR KNOT – This is another general-purpose knot that also offersmaximumstrength and versatility. The palomar knot is dependable and easy to tie, and it's a good alternative to the Trilene knot.

To tie the palomar knot, bend the line back on itself to form a double strand 6 inches long. Pass this double strand through the hook eye, and tie a loose overhand knot, leaving a loop deep enough so the hook (or lure) can pass through it. Pass the hook through the loop, then tighten the knot by pulling the hook with one hand and the double strand of line with the other. Trim the tag end.

IMPROVED CLINCH KNOT – This is a third general-purpose knot that is an old standby in fishing. It's slightly weaker than the

PALOMAR KNOT

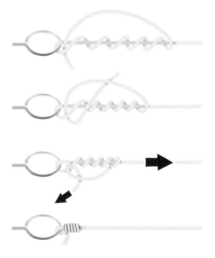

IMPROVED CLINCH KNOT

SURGEON'S LOOP

Trilene or palomar knot, but it's still strong and easy enough to tie to be the choice of many expert anglers.

To tie the improved clinch knot, thread the line through the hook eye 3-4 inches. Wrap the end of the line around the standing line 6 times. Then run the end back through the opening between the hook and the first wrap. Last, turn the end up and thread it through the long loop between the wraps and the downturned line. Hold onto the end and snug the line by pulling the standing line and hook in opposite directions. Clip the tag end. (Note: some experts double their line and tie this knot as if their doubled line was a single strand.)

SURGEON'S LOOP – When you want to tie a loop in your line, this is the knot to use. The surgeon's loop knot is easy to tie, and it won't slip.

To tie the surgeon's loop knot, bend the line back to double it. Then tie a simple overhand knot. Instead of snugging this knot up tight, make another wrap in the

overhand knot. Now snug the knot tight and clip the tag end.

BLOOD KNOT – The blood knot is good for adding new line to old line on your reel. This knot requires a fair amount of practice to learn,

BLOOD KNOT

because it's easy to get the twists and ends confused. However, once you master it, you can splice two lines together quickly and securely.

To tie the blood knot, overlap the two lines 4-5 inches end to end. Wrap one around the other 5 times. Next, wrap the second line around the first line 5 times in the opposite direction. Last, pass both ends back through the center opening in opposite directions. While holding these tag ends, snug the line up tight. Then trim the ends.

LINE END KNOT – This knot is used for tying line to an empty reel spool. It's simple and allows the line to slide down snug against the spool so it won't slip.

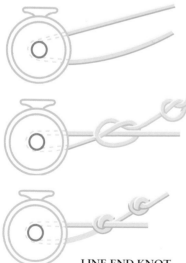

LINE END KNOT

Begin by looping the line around the reel spool. Then tie a simple overhand knot around the standing line to form a slip knot. Last, tie another overhand knot in the end of the line to anchor the slip knot when the line is drawn tight. Snug the line tightly around the reel spool and trim the tag end.

Hooks, Sinkers, Floats

Hooks, sinkers and floats are basic components in many fishing rigs. Different combinations of hooks, sinkers and floats can be used on everything from small panfish to large gamefish. These items of "terminal tackle" come in many different sizes and designs. Beginning anglers must understand these differences, and must learn to select and assemble the right tackle for the species they're targeting.

Hooks: Getting to the Point

Hooks can be confusing to expert anglers, much less beginners. One major manufacturer makes hooks in more than 40,000 designs, sizes and finishes. They run the gamut from tiny wire hooks for trout to giant forged hooks for such saltwater brutes as sharks and marlin. Hooks also come in different

Hook Selection

Following are recommendations for hook sizes and styles for popular fish species. In each case, the range of sizes given will work for the fish in question. For general-purpose use, the best selection for each species would be the medium-sized hook in the category. However, if you know your fish are likely to be on the small size, or if you're fishing strictly for trophy fish, adjust your hook choice down or up accordingly.

One special note should be made about camshaft hooks. These hooks have offset bends in the shaft. When a fish bites down on the offset, the hook's point rotates to a better penetrating angle, making it easier to get a solid hookset. These hooks really work! I recommend them when fishing with live bait, plastic worms and in other single-hook situations.

Overall, don't worry about different names and styles of hooks. Again, many different hooks will serve the same purpose. Just find one design and size for the type fishing you'll be doing. If it works, stick with it. Later on you might want to learn more about hook styles and the subtle differences in each. But for now, stick with the basics, and you'll be okay.

BASS
Sizes #2-4/0.
When using live bait, choose smaller wire hooks. When using plastic worms or other artificial lures, use 1/0-4/0 forged steel hooks.

SUNFISH
Sizes #10-#6 light wire hooks.
Hooks with a long shank are better, since they are easier to remove when a sunfish swallows the live bait.

CRAPPIE/WHITE BASS
Sizes #4-2/0 light wire hooks.

WALLEYE/SAUGER
Sizes #6-#1 light wire hooks.
Some experts prefer "baitholder" hooks when using minnows, nightcrawlers or leeches.

YELLOW PERCH
#8-#4 light wire hooks.

MUSKELLUNGE/PIKE
Sizes 1/0-6/0 forged steel hooks.

STREAMTROUT
Sizes #10-#1 Aberdeen or "baitholder" hooks.

STRIPED BASS/HYBRIDS
Sizes 1/0-6/0 forged steel hooks.

LARGE CATFISH
Sizes 1/0-7/0 forged steel hooks. Sizes #8-#1 light wire hooks.

thicknesses, temper (springiness), barb configurations and other features. Different styles of hooks bear different names: Aberdeen, O'Shaughnessy, Carlisle, Limerick, etc. (Modern hook making originated in the British Isles, where these hooks were named.) With so many variables, it's easy to understand how a beginning angler can feel intimidated when faced with choosing just the right hook. Don't worry! You do not have to become a hook expert to be a successful angler. Making good hook selections is easy if you follow a few basic guidelines.

First, buy quality hooks, not the bargain-basement variety. Stick with popular brand names that are most widely advertised and distributed. Quality hooks cost only slightly more than inferior ones, and they're more than worth the price in terms of strength and reliability.

Second, pay special attention to hook size. The simple rule is to use small hooks for small fish and big hooks for big fish. As logical as this seems, this is a common mistake made by beginning anglers. They use bass-size hooks when fishing for small panfish, and the little fish can't get the hook in their mouths.

It's important to understand the system manufacturers use to label hook sizes. Smaller hooks are "number-sized," the larger its number, the smaller the hook. For instance, a #32 hook is tiny and used in small flies. A #10 hook is much larger and might be suitable for bluegill or perch. A #1 hook is larger still and a good size for crappie, walleye, small bass and catfish.

At this point, numbering switches over to the "aught" system and heads in the other direction. After a #1 hook, the next largest size is a 1/0 (pronounced "one-aught"), followed by 2/0, 3/0 and so on. These larger hooks are used for bigger bass and catfish, pike, muskies, stripers, lake trout, etc.

The following chart will guide you in selecting hooks for specific fish.

Sinkers: A "Weighty" Matter

Sinkers are weights that pull the bait down to the level the angler desires. Sinkers are molded – typically from lead – in many different designs and sizes. The type sinker you use and how you use it depends on what rig and technique you select for the species you're

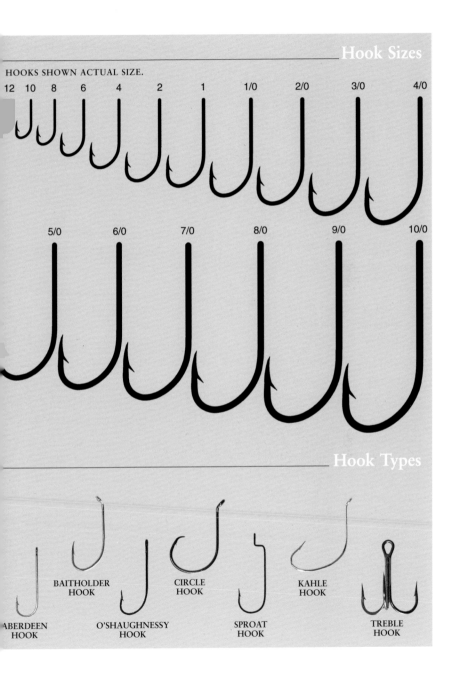

HOOKS SHOWN ACTUAL SIZE.

12   10   8   6   4   2   1   1/0   2/0   3/0   4/0

5/0   6/0   7/0   8/0   9/0   10/0

BAITHOLDER
HOOK

CIRCLE
HOOK

KAHLE
HOOK

ABERDEEN
HOOK

O'SHAUGHNESSY
HOOK

SPROAT
HOOK

TREBLE
HOOK

after. In terms of size, use a sinker heavy enough to do the job, but no heavier than it has to be. In most cases, the lighter the sinker, the less noticeable it will be to the fish.

The most common sinkers are those that clamp directly onto the line. Split shot are small round balls that are pinched onto the line along a slit through the middle of the sinker. Clincher sinkers are elongated weights that pinch onto the line. Rubbercor sinkers resemble clinchers, but they have a rubber strip through the center. Line is looped behind this rubber to hold the sinker in place.

Sliding sinkers have holes through the middle so the line can slide freely through them. Three common examples are the egg sinker and the bullet sinker (named for their shape) and the walking slip sinker, named for the special way it's used. Egg sinkers are used with stationary live bait

rigs. The most common use for bullet sinkers is with Texas-rigged plastic worms. And walking slip sinkers are used with slip-sinker rigs to crawl live bait across the bottom.

Various other sinkers are used with bottom-bumping or stationary rigs. Bell swivel sinkers are bell-shaped and have a brass swivel molded in. The line is tied to the swivel, which prevents line twist when you're drift-fishing or bottom-bouncing. Bank sinkers are general purpose bottom sinkers which cast well, slide easily along smooth bottoms and hold well in current. Pyramid and inverted pyramid sinkers have sharp edges and flat sides for gripping in soft, smooth bottoms.

There are many other sinkers for special techniques such as trolling and drifting. But the sinkers listed above are the ones used in the rigs outlined later in this chapter

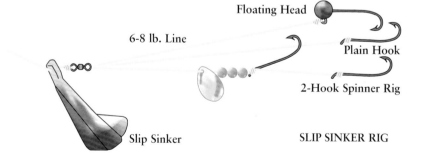

Floating Head

6-8 lb. Line

Plain Hook

2-Hook Spinner Rig

Slip Sinker

SLIP SINKER RIG

and also in the fishing techniques described in Chapter 8.

Floats: Visual Strike Indicators

Most fishermen start out as bobber fishermen. They watch a float with a bait suspended beneath it, and they wait for a fish to pull the float under. This is a very simple yet effective and exciting way to fish.

Floats actually serve two purposes. The first is to suspend the bait at whatever depth the angler wishes, and the second is to signal when a bite is occurring. A float holds the bait as shallow or deep as you desire. It allows you to dangle the bait just above bottom or suspend it over the top of brush, submerged weeds or other underwater cover.

Also, if you want to fish close to the bottom, but you don't know how deep it is, the float can tell you. If your sinker is resting on bottom, there's no weight pulling against the float, so it will lie on its side on the surface. But when you shorten the length of line between your float and sinker so the sinker is no longer touching bottom, the pull will cause the float to ride upright. Then, knowing that your bait is a set distance below your

Size 6 Eagle Claw Salmon Hook

30" or 48"
Six Pound Test Snell

Barrel Swivel

⅛-½ oz.
Slip Sinker

SLIP SINKER RIG

sinker (i.e., 6 inches), you know how deep your bait is and its position relative to the bottom.

Floats come in many materials, shapes and sizes. Most floats are made from hard plastic, foam plastic, buoyant wood, cork or porcupine quills. Float designs include round, tubular, barrel-shaped, pearshaped, quill-shaped, and combinations of these designs.

Long, slender floats are more sensitive to light bites than round ones. Slender floats cast better since there's less wind resistance. I recommend them over round floats for most small-bait, light-tackle situations. If you're fishing for larger fish with larger baits, sensitivity isn't so critical, and round floats will work fine. Also, a good compromise for general use is the combination of a round or barrel float with a quill-like stem running through the middle. The thick part provides plenty of buoyancy for the sinker/hook/bait, while the quill adds sensitivity to indicate that you're getting a bite.

Most floats attach onto the line with a small, spring-loaded wire clip. Others are pegged onto the line. A third family of floats slides up and down the line freely.

Many beginning anglers make the mistake of fishing with a float that's too large. Select a float that's the smallest possible size considering the weight of your sinker, hook and bait. You want the float to ride high on the surface, but the slightest tug should pull it under. If a float is too large, smaller fish will have trouble swimming down with the bait. This unnatural resistance from the float may alert them to danger. So keep several different-sized floats in your tackle box to match different fishing conditions and rigs.

Snaps, Swivels, Snap Swivels, Split Rigs and Leaders

Snaps, swivels, snap swivels, split rings and leaders are additional types of terminal tackle for use with various rigs and lures.

A snap is a small wire bracket with a safety-pin catch. It's simply a device for changing lures or hooks faster and easier. Tie the line to one end and snap the lure on the other end. To change lures, simply unsnap the catch, take the old lure off, put the new one on, and fasten the catch back. With a snap, you don't have to cut and retie line each time you change lures.

There are tradeoffs for this convenience, however. A snap adds more weight, drag, and hardware that the fish might see. Also, snaps occasionally bend or break under pressure from hard-fighting fish. For these reasons, I rarely use a snap. Instead, I prefer to tie my line directly to the eye of the hook or lure. The only time I use a snap is when I know I'll need to change lures frequently. When I do use a snap, I choose the smallest, lightest one possible, considering the size and strength of the fish I'm after.

A swivel is a small revolving metal link that's often tied between the main line and other components of terminal rig. A swivel prevents line twist caused by rotating lures or natural baits. Like snaps, swivels also have drawbacks. One

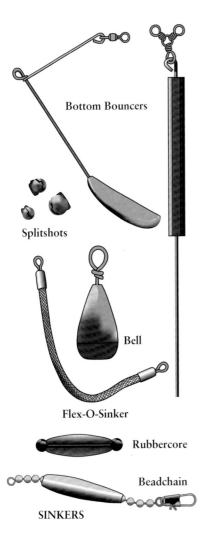

Bottom Bouncers

Splitshots

Bell

Flex-O-Sinker

Rubbercore

Beadchain

SINKERS

The "three-way swivel" is an important specialty swivel. As its name describes, it has three tie-on rings instead of two. This swivel is used in the bottom-fishing rig described in the next section of this chapter.

A snap swivel is a combination of a snap and a swivel. Many fishermen use snap swivels with all types of rigs and lures. In most cases, however, they're unnecessary and even ill-advised. Snap swivels add weight, which can deaden the action of a lure. They can create a weak link between line and hook and increase the chance of fouling on brush or weeds. I only use a snap swivel for casting in-line (revolving) spinners with spinning tackle.

The split ring is a small over-lapping wire ring threaded into the eye of a lure – the line is tied to the ring. This is to allow more freedom of movement in the lure, which gives a more lifelike action. Many lures come from the factory with a split ring pre-attached. If a lure doesn't have a split ring, I don't add one. Some lures perform better with the line tied directly to the eye. Also, I never clip a snap swivel into a split ring. Such a connection hampers lure action.

main drawback is poor design or material that keeps the swivel from rotating freely. The best swivels are ballbearing swivels that revolve under far less pressure than swivels without ball bearings. I strongly recommend them.

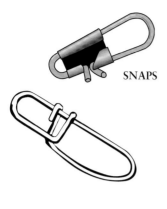

SPLIT RING

THREE-WAY SWIVELS

SWIVELS

A leader is a length of fishing line or thin wire tied or fastened between the main line and the hook/lure. Leaders serve either of two main purposes: (1) increase line strength next to the hook; (2) provide a low-visibility connection between a highly visible main line and the bait. This keeps the visible line from scaring fish, and it also makes the bait look more natural.

The term "leader" also means an additional length of line tied into a terminal rig for adding extra hooks. This is the most common use of leaders for beginning fishermen.

Most leaders are monofilament. Thin wire leaders, however, are used by anglers trying for toothy fish like pike and muskies that can bite monofilament in two.

Rigs for Everyday Fishing

Now we get to the heart of the matter. You know enough about hooks, sinkers, floats, knots and other terminal tackle to start assembling different rigs for specific fishing situations. Following are explanations and diagrams of 9 basic rigs, including how to tie them and where and how to use them. Sizes of hooks, sinkers, floats and lines in these rigs will

Fixed-Bobber Rig

This is the old standby float/sinker/hook rig that catches almost anything that swims. It's used mainly in calm water (ponds, lakes, rivers or pools of streams). It works with both poles and casting tackle, although it's awkward to cast with more than three feet of line between the bobber and hook.

To assemble this rig, first tie the hook to the end of the line. Next, fasten a split shot, clincher or Rubbercor sinker 6 inches up the line. Clamp or wrap the sinker tightly onto the line so it won't slip down. Last, attach a bobber onto the line at the desired distance above the sinker. The bobber can be adjusted up or down the line to float the bait at whatever depth you desire.

The fixed-bobber rig is extremely easy to use. When a fish is nibbling, the bobber will twitch on the surface. When the fish takes the bait, the bobber will move away fast or be yanked underwater. That's the time to set the hook!

Always balance the size of the sinker and float. Use just enough sinker to take the bait down, then match this with a float barely large enough to hang on the surface, holding up the weight of the sinker

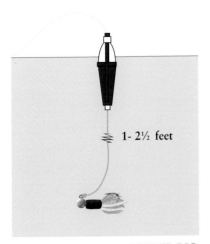

1- 2½ feet

FIXED BOBBER RIG

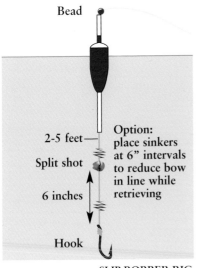

Bead

2-5 feet

Split shot

6 inches

Option:
place sinkers
at 6" intervals
to reduce bow
in line while
retrieving

Hook

SLIP BOBBER RIG

vary from one fishing situation to the next, depending on size and strength of target fish, water depth, bottom type, amount of current and other variables.

and bait. This way, even the slightest tug from a fish will pull the float under.

Slip-Bobber Rig

The slip-bobber rig is so-named because the bobber slides freely up and down the line. It allows you to cast from shore or boat and offer the bait at any desired length.

The slip-bobber rig is similar to the fixed-bobber rig, with the exception of the free-sliding bobber. The bobber is run up the line first. (The line runs through the middle of the bobber.) Next, attach a sinker 6 inches up the line. The bobber will slide down and rest atop the sinker. Then tie the hook on the end of the line. Last, a "bobber stop" is attached to the line above the bobber that gives the depth where you want to fish. For instance, to fish 5 feet deep, tie the bobber stop 5 feet up the line from the hook.

Some float rigs are sold with a bobber stop in a package. The stop is typically a short piece of plastic tube with thread tied loosely around the tube. To use this stop, run it up the line first, then follow with the float, sinker and hook as described above. Another form of bobber stop can be a piece of

rubber band tied tightly around the line.

When casting with a slip-bobber rig, the bobber, sinker, hook and bait are near the end of the line, which makes casting easy. When the rig hits the water, the weight of the sinker and hook sink pull line through the bobber until it hits the stop. Again, fishing depth may be altered by raising or lowering the bobber stop on the line.

Bottom Rig

This is the basic rig for fishing on bottom without a float. Bottom rigs are mainly used for catfish and bullheads, but they also work on bottom-feeding bass, walleye, trout and other species. A bottom rig works in both quiet water and current.

This rig is built around a three-way swivel. Tie the main line into one ring of the swivel. Tie a 12-inch leader on the second ring of the swivel, and tie a bank or bell swivel sinker on the other end of this leader. Last, tie an 18-inch leader into the third ring of the swivel. The hook and bait go on the end of this leader.

The bottom rig is highly versatile. It can be used from shore or boat, with light or heavy tackle.

Length of the leaders for the sinker and hook/bait may be altered as desired. Typically, though, the hook leader should be longer than the sinker leader.

Since you don't use a float with this rig, how can you tell when you're getting a bite? With the sinker resting on bottom, reel up slack until the line is taut to the rod tip. Then, if you're holding the rod, you'll feel the bite. If the rod is propped up, you'll see the tip jerk. Some fishermen attach small bells to their rod tips to alert them to bites. Also, your line may start moving as a fish swims off with the bait. The key to using a bottom rig is keeping slack out of the line so you'll notice these things.

Live-Bait Rig

This is a stationary rig that allows natural action from live bait. It can be used in any type water and for a wide variety of fish.

To tie this rig, run a sliding egg sinker up the line. Now clamp on a BB-size split shot sinker below the egg sinker and 18 inches up from the end of the line. This split

shot serves as a stop to keep the egg sinker from riding down on the bait. Last, tie the hook on the end of the line, and bait it with a minnow, crawfish or night crawler. Now the bait can swim freely off bottom and pull line through the sinker. Also, when a fish takes the bait, it can swim off without feeling the unnatural weight of the sinker.

Slip-Sinker Rig

Also called the "walking-sinker rig," this rig is used to pull live bait across the bottom, either by trolling or casting and slowly cranking in line. This rig is highly effective on walleye, but it can also be used for many other species.

Most slip-sinker rigs are sold in packages, but they can also be assembled from individual components. First, slide a walking-type sinker up the line, then tie on a small barrel swivel. Tie a 3-foot monofilament leader onto the other end of the barrel swivel, and add the hook at the end of this leader. (Many pre-tied slip-sinker rigs have a spinner blade in front of the

3-4 feet
Bait doctor   Rapala

LIVE BAIT RIG   **BOTTOM BOUNCING RIG**   **BOTTOM RIG**

hook.) Bait with a night crawler, leech, crawfish or minnow.

Most experts troll or drag slip-sinker rigs with spinning tackle. When a fish takes the bait, they trip the bail and give line freely so the fish can run. When the run stops, they reel in slack line until they feel pressure on the line, then they set the hook!

Bottom-Bouncing Rig

Bottom bouncers are weighted wire devices used to troll baits along snaggy bottoms. Thin steel wire is bent into an "L" shape. A lead weight is molded around the center of the long arm. The short arm has a ring for tying on a 3-foot leader and hook. The main line is tied into the 90-degree bend of the "L," between the bottom bouncer's two arms.

The bottom bouncer is mainly used when fishing from a boat. It is lowered to the bottom and then pulled slowly through likely structure. Enough line should be let out so the bottom bouncer is trailing well behind the boat. The wire holds the weight up off bottom where it won't hang up, and the leader and baited hook float behind, just above the bottom.

The bottom bouncer is used mainly for walleye, but it's also extremely effective on bass, crappie, catfish and other structure-oriented species.

Two-Hook Panfish Rig

This is a deep-water rig used primarily for crappie and catfish. It is fished "tightline" fashion (no float) from a boat. The sinker is on the bottom of this rig, and it's jigged slowly off bottom while two baited hooks dangle above it. Minnows are the usual bait for this rig, though small crappie jigs may also be used.

First, tie a bell swivel sinker to the end of the line. Next, tie a surgeon's knot 18 inches above the swivel to form a loop that is big enough to stretch 3 inches. Now tie an identical loop 18 inches up from this first loop. Last, add hooks to the loops in the followingmanner. Pinch the loop closely together so the line is doubled, then run it through the eye of a thin wire hook (#2-1/0). Then open the loop and pull the hook back through it. Slide the hook tight at the end of the loop, and add bait.

Texas-Rigged Plastic Worm

Plastic worms are popular among bass fishermen, and the Texas-rigged

TYING A SPREADER RIG

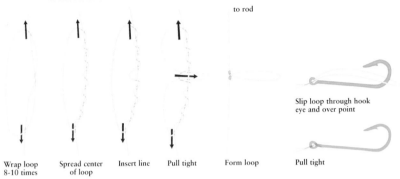

to rod

Slip loop through hook
eye and over point

Wrap loop 8-10 times | Spread center of loop | Insert line | Pull tight

Form loop | Pull tight

worm is the favorite way to use this bait. A Texas-rigged worm is weedless and can be crawled through thick cover where bass like to hide.

Start by running a sliding bullet sinker up the line (⅛-⅜ ounce for depths up to 10 feet), then tie on a plastic worm hook. Insert the point of the hook ½ inch into the head of the worm. Now pull the point out the side of the worm, and slide the worm up the shank of the hook until the eye is pulled into the head of the worm. Last, rotate the hook and reinsert the point into the side of the worm, completely covering the barb. Done correctly, the worm will hang straight with the hook in place.

Rigged in this manner, the sinker will slide freely along the line. Many anglers prefer to peg the sinker at the head of the worm. This can be done by using a "screw-in" sinker (molded-in screw anchors the sinker to the head of the worm) or by pushing the small point of a flat toothpick through the hole of a regular bullet sinker, from the back toward the front. When the toothpick can be pushed no further, break it off even with the bottom of the sinker. Then slide the sinker down the line to the head of the worm, and it'll stay in place.

A special section on how to fish Texas-rigged plastic worms is included in the next chapter.

Carolina-Rigged Plastic Worm

Where the Texas-rigged worm is meant for fishing in heavy cover,

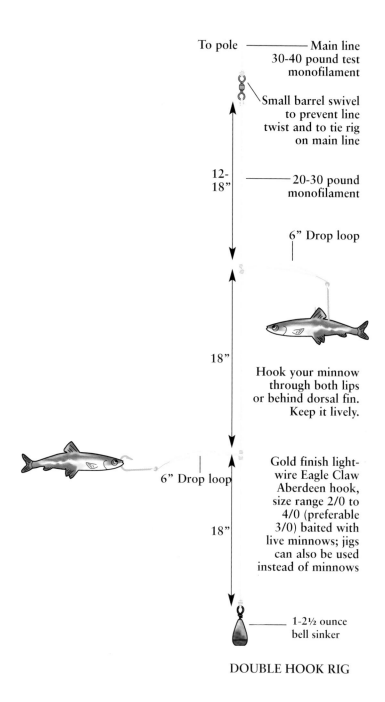

To pole ——— Main line
30-40 pound test
monofilament

Small barrel swivel
to prevent line
twist and to tie rig
on main line

12-
18" ——— 20-30 pound
monofilament

6" Drop loop

18"

Hook your minnow
through both lips
or behind dorsal fin.
Keep it lively.

6" Drop loop

Gold finish light-
wire Eagle Claw
Aberdeen hook,
size range 2/0 to
4/0 (preferable
3/0) baited with
live minnows; jigs
can also be used
instead of minnows

18"

1-2½ ounce
bell sinker

DOUBLE HOOK RIG

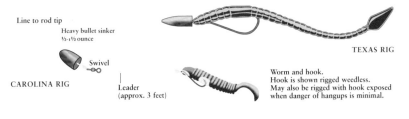

Line to rod tip

Heavy bullet sinker
½-1½ ounce

Swivel

CAROLINA RIG

Leader
(approx. 3 feet)

TEXAS RIG

Worm and hook.
Hook is shown rigged weedless.
May also be rigged with hook exposed
when danger of hangups is minimal.

the Carolina-rigged worm is designed for open structure fishing and covering long distances of a submerged channel dropoff, sunken point, bank, etc. It's very similar to the live-bait rig, except it uses a plastic worm for bait. It's also a very easy rig to use. You simply make a long cast, allow the rig to sink to bottom, then crank it back in very slowly. There are two basic presentations: dragging - pulling sideways with the rod tip; and small hops by making vertical lifts with the rod tip.

To make a Carolina rig, run a heavy bullet slip sinker (½-1 ounce) up the line; then tie a barrel swivel

Using the proper rig is crucial in fishing. Anglers who know how to match and adjust rigs to particular fishing situations will get more action than those who don't

on the end of the line. Next, tie a
3-foot leader with a hook and plastic worm or lizard on the end. With
this rig, the bait is usually fished
with the point exposed. Do this by
inserting the point of the hook into
the head of the worm/lizard and
then threading the worm around
the bend of the hook and up the
shaft. Last, pull the point out the
top of the bait, and pull the bait up
to straighten it. Properly done, the
worm/lizard should hang straight
on the hook. (Some anglers rig
the hook weedless when fishing in
snaggy cover.)

Summary

Entire books have been written
about fishing rigs, so it's difficult to
cover this subject in a single chapter. However, you can use these 9
rigs in probably 90% of freshwater fishing in North America. These
rigs are versatile and productive!
Pick the ones that apply to the type
fishing you do, then practice tying
and using them until they become
second nature.

In the next chapter you'll learn
about baits, and in Chapter 8 we'll
cover easy fishing techniques for
different spots. These three chapters – 6, 7 and 8 – are the heart
and soul of Basic Fishing. Study
them carefully, and follow their
tips. If you use the right rig, bait
and methods in a location where
fish exist, you'll catch some almost
every time. You'll also have learned
the basics, and you'll be ready to
progress to a higher level of fishing
knowledge and skills.

CHAPTER 7

Natural Bait
and Artificial Lures

O ne of my most vivid fishing memories is of a Sunday afternoon in springtime when I was in grade school. After church and family dinner, I headed off fishing in a large pond on our neighbor's farm. I'd trapped some minnows for bait. (Our family raised and sold minnows for extra income.) My plan was to use a long cane pole to bobber-fish for crappie.

Successful fishing depends upon being able to pick the right bait or lure for the situation at hand. A beginning angler must learn about different baits/lures and how to make the best possible selection for his target species and water conditions.

However, as I eased up to the water's edge, I spied a large bass finning lazily in the shallows below me. I crept backward, unwound the line from my pole, and baited my hook with the biggest minnow in the bucket. Then I eased back to the pond's edge and lowered the minnow right in front of the bass' nose.

Suddenly I had a tempest on my line! The bass inhaled the minnow and hooked itself in the process. The fish went wild, jumping and thrashing and splashing water and mud in all directions. I held on and was finally able to drag that fish out on the bank. That was enough action for one day! I headed straight home to show my catch. In less than a half-hour I was back with a 5-pound largemouth and a memory to keep forever.

In this case, the big minnow did the trick. At other times it was worms, crawfish and other live or artificial baits. Bait is a part of every fishing story. This is why beginners must learn about different baits, which work on which species, and how to use them. Simply put, if you're not savvy about baits, you won't catch many fish.

Natural and Artificial Baits

There are two broad categories of baits: natural and artificial.

Natural baits are organic. They include minnows, worms, insects, crawfish, leeches, frogs, cut bait (fish pieces) – a wide variety of living or once-living critters.

Artificial baits include a vast range of lures. Some mimic natural bait. Others bear no resemblance to any natural food, yet they have some attraction that causes fish to bite. (Besides being hungry, fish strike artificial lures because they're mad, greedy, curious or impulsive.)

The list of categories of artificial baits includes topwaters, spinners, crankbaits, soft plastics, jigs, spoons and flies. Further, these categories can be broken down into individual types of baits. For example, soft plastics include plastic worms, lizards, grubs, crawfish, tubes, eels, minnows and more.

Natural baits are effective on most species of fish. Minnows, worms, grasshoppers, crawfish, leeches, and other "critters" offer real look, movement and smell, and feeding fish bite them with little hesitation

So, which should you use: natural bait or artificials? Anglers have faced this decision since the first artificial lures were invented. (Before this, natural baits were the only choice.) Basically, this is a matter of personal preference, convenience, and bait capabilities. Each has certain advantages over the other.

Fish usually prefer natural bait over artificials. A bluegill will eat a real earthworm before it will a plastic one. If a live crawfish is retrieved next to an artificial crawfish, a bass will recognize and take the live one. These are examples of why more fish caught in North America are taken on natural bait. It's hard to beat Mother Nature.

So why even bother with artificial baits? There are several reasons. First, many anglers enjoy the challenge of using artificials. Since fish are harder to catch on artificials, these anglers feel there's more reward in fooling the fish with them. These people are fishing more for sport than for meat.

Second, artificial baits are more convenient. You don't have to dig or trap them, and you don't have to keep them alive and fresh. Most can be kept in a tackle box indefinitely and fished with no advance preparation.

Third, artificial lures have certain capabilities and attractions that natural baits don't have. While natural baits are normally used with a stationary or slow-moving presentation, artificials may be retrieved fast to cover a lot of water quickly. They sometimes

Ethics & Etiquette

*Leave It As You Found It!
Don't litter. Never leave trash on the shore, toss it out of the boat or car window or sink cans in the water. Don't leave anything behind after a day's fishing except footprints in the mud or sand.*

Many anglers find success using the specific live bait upon which their target fish are feeding. For instance, small shad, like the one shown at left, are a favorite target of game- and panfish. Capture some alive, hook one on and offer it where fish are feeding, and chances are very good for a strike!

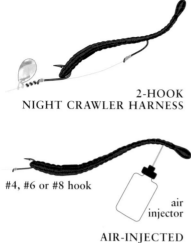

**2-HOOK
NIGHT CRAWLER HARNESS**

#4, #6 or #8 hook

air
injector

**AIR-INJECTED
NIGHT CRAWLER**

cause inactive fish to strike out of impulse or anger as the bait runs by (the "catch-itbefore- it-gets-away" syndrome). On the other hand, this same fish might ignore a minnow hanging under a bobber.

So, when deciding which to use, weigh the advantages of natural bait versus artificials as they relate to your particular fishing situation. Which is more important: making a good catch, or enjoying a sporty challenge? How difficult is it to get and keep natural bait?Which type bait is more likely to suit your fish's mood and location and the technique you'll use to try for it?

Using Natural Bait

To use natural bait, you have to get it, keep it fresh, hook it on properly, and offer it with the right presentation. Following are guidelines for fishing with several popular natural baits.

But first, although the following outlines tell you how to catch your own bait, in many cases it's more practical to buy bait from a bait/tackle dealer. True, catching bait can be almost as much fun as catching fish, but I usually buy my bait to save as much time as possible for fooling the fish.

One other note: fish normally prefer fresh, active bait to old, lifeless bait. This is why I always keep fresh bait on my hook. If my minnow quits swimming, I replace it with a new one!

WORMS – Worms are the most popular of all natural baits. They include large night crawlers and

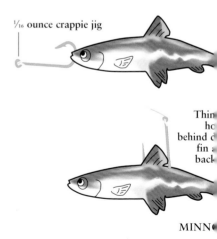

¹⁄₁₆ ounce crappie jig

Thin
ho
behind d
fin a
back

MINN

Lures come in every color, shade and pattern imaginable. Manufacturers use colors to capture the fancy of anglers who buy their lures. Less-experienced anglers almost always ask what color lure another fisherman used to make a good catch. We're tuned in to colors, and I think we give lure color more credit than it deserves in fishing success.

I do pay attention to color, but I don't think it's critical in making a good catch. That said, I've seen times when fish were very color-specific. They wanted one color and nothing else. Still, for those few times, I've seen many more when the fish would hit any of several colors presented to them.

When choosing lure color, I normally stick to what's natural to the fish. If they're feeding on shad, I'll use a shad-colored lure. If they're feeding on crawfish, I want a bait with an orange belly and brown or green back.

There are exceptions to this rule. If the water is muddy, I prefer bright lures that show up better in the murk. If the water is clear, I favor white or chrome crankbaits and spinners or translucent soft plastic baits.

Again, seek advice about lure colors for particular lakes or reservoirs. But stick with the basic colors, and concentrate more on fish location and depth.

---

a variety of smaller earthworms ("wigglers"). Worms can be used to catch a variety of panfish and sportfish. They're especially good on catfish, bullheads, bass, sunfish, walleye, yellow perch and trout.

Worms are easy to collect. You can dig for them in moist, rich soil in gardens, around barnyards, and under rotting leaves or logs. Night crawlers can be collected on a grassy lawn at night following a warm rain. Place freshly-captured worms in a small container partially filled with loose crumbled dirt. If you put a top on the container, make sure it has holes so the worms can breathe.

Keep the worm can or box out of the sun so the worms won't overheat and die. Many anglers keep their worms in a cooler. If you have leftover worms, they will keep for several days in a refrigerator.

There are several methods for using worms. With a stationary rig (bobber rig, bottom rig), gob one or more worms onto the hook, running the point through the middle of the worm's body several times with the ends dangling free. When fishing for small sunfish or yellow perch, don't put too much worm on the hook, since these fish have small mouths. But when fishing for catfish, bass and other large fish, the more worms on the hook, the better.

If you're fishing for walleye or bass with a walking slip-sinker or a bottom bouncer, hook the worm (normally a night crawler) once through the head so the body can trail out behind. When driftfishing in a stream for trout, hook the worm through the middle of the body and allow the two ends to dangle.

MINNOWS – Shiners, tuffies (fatheads) and goldfish are popular minnow species that are sold in bait stores. Also, other small minnows can be caught from ponds, streams and lakes. Anglers routinely use minnows to catch crappie, bass, walleye, sauger, catfish, white bass, stripers and other fish.

One of the easiest ways to catch minnows is to set a wire basket trap. (Most tackle stores sell these traps.) Bait the trap with a piece of bread and drop it into a pond or creek where minnows live. Leave it for a few hours, then retrieve it with its catch inside. Minnows may also be seined or caught with a cast net. However, seines and nets are expensive, and both take a fair amount of know-how to use. For these reasons, I don't recommend them for beginning fishermen.

Small minnows are effective on crappie, bass, white bass and other species. Always keep a lively minnow on the hook. If a minnow dies or tires out, replace it with a fresh, wiggly one.

Minnows must be cared for properly, or they will die quickly. Keep their water cool and fresh. I use Styrofoam buckets instead of metal or plastic, because Styrofoam keeps the water cooler. I never put more than 4 dozen minnows in a bucket to avoid overcrowding. If the water in a bucket becomes too warm or stale (oxygen is running out), the minnows will rise to the surface, and you must take quick action to save them. Exchange the old water for fresh. On extremely hot days, add chunks of ice to keep the water cool. And you might consider purchasing a small battery-powered bait aerator to spray water into the bucket to maintain a good oxygen supply.

Minnows can be kept several days between trips. Store them in the refrigerator and change their water as often as needed.

When I fish with minnows, I put them on the hook two ways. If I'm using a stationary rig, I hook the minnow through the back under the main fin. This allows it to swim naturally. But if I'm using a moving rig like a bottom-bouncer, walking slip sinker or two-hook rig, I hook the minnow through both lips, from bottom to top. And again, I frequently replace battered or dead minnows with fresh ones. New minnows always attract more bites than used ones.

CRICKETS/GRASSHOPPERS – Crickets and grasshoppers are excellent baits for sunfish, bass, catfish and trout.

You can catch grasshoppers in grassy or weedy fields either by hand or with a butterfly net. Or better yet, you and a friend can open a fuzzy wool blanket and run through a field into the wind. The grasshoppers will try to fly away, but the wind will blow them into the blanket, and their legs will stick in the fuzz. To catch crickets, look under rocks, planks or logs, and grab them by hand or with a net. (Watch out for poisonous spiders and snakes when doing this!)

Place grasshoppers or crickets in a cricket box from a tackle store, or make your own container by punching holes in a coffee can that has a plastic lid. Cut a small round hole in the lid, and keep it covered with masking tape. Peel the tape back to deposit grasshoppers or crickets as you catch them. When you want to get one out, peel the tape back, shake an insect out of the hole, then stick the tape back over the hole.

Grasshoppers and crickets should be stored in a cool, shady place. Each day add a damp paper towel for moisture and a tablespoon of corn meal for food.

Grasshoppers and crickets are normally used with bobber rigs or bottom rigs. They are hooked by inserting the point behind the tail and running it the length of the body and out at the head.

CRICKET

CRAWFISH

CRAWFISH – Crawfish are found in most freshwater lakes and streams. Many anglers think of them as good bass baits (smallmouth love them!), but they are also deadly on catfish. Pieces of crawfish tail are irresistible to sunfish.

The best way to gather crawfish is to go wading in a shallow stream and slowly turn over flat rocks. When you see a crawfish, ease a tin can (with holes punched in the bottom) up behind it, and then poke at its head with a stick. Crawfish swim backward to escape, so it should back up into the can. When the crawfish goes in, lift the can quickly.

Keep crawfish in a Styrofoam minnow bucket half-filled with water. They can be kept several days if refrigerated.

When handling crawfish, be careful to avoid their pinchers, which can cause painful injury. Hold them by the body just behind the pinchers.

Live crawfish should be hooked in the back section of the tail, from the bottom through the top. They are usually fished on or near bottom with a standard bottom rig or live-bait rig. They can also be trolled slowly along bottom with a slip-sinker rig or bottom bouncer. And once in awhile, they should be fished just above bottom with a bobber rig.

A broad variety of natural baits can be collected from nature. For instance, in late spring, large yellow-and-black worms infest catalpa trees in many regions, and these worms are a choice food for catfish. They can't resist them!

Making Sense Out of Fish Scent

Tackle store shelves are lined with scent products designed to make fish bite more eagerly and to hold onto a bait longer. These products come in two forms: scent-impregnated baits (the scent is molded into the bait); and add-on scents, which are applied to baits either by spraying or smearing on.

Do these products really work? This is a difficult question. My best answer is, some probably work some of the time, and some better than others. Confusing?

Biologists know that many fish species have a well-developed sense of smell. Also, testing by independent laboratories indicates that scent application sometimes increases the chance that fish will bite and hold onto a lure longer.

However, scent products aren't magic potions that will cause inactive fish to suddenly go into a feeding frenzy. A scent may persuade a borderline fish that's inspecting a bait to bite it. But don't expect miracles to happen if you start using scents or scented lures.

In my opinion, scents are most effective when used on slow moving artificial baits like plastic worms, jigs, grubs, etc. I don't use them on fast-moving baits like crankbaits and spinnerbaits. These are more visual/reaction baits. Fish don't have time to sniff them before they decide to bite or let them pass.

However, with slower-moving baits, fish may have a chance to follow, observe and smell. A natural or inviting smell may add just enough persuasion to cause a curious or undecided fish to feed. Or, if it bites into a plastic worm, lizard, crawfish or whatever with scent impregnated, and it gets a pleasing taste, the fish might hold on longer, allowing the angler more time to set the hook.

I can't say with 100% certainty that scents have ever helped me, but I think they have. Each angler has to decide for himself whether or not to use scent products. The fishing-scent industry is built on the basis that scents may help anglers increase their catch. If you experiment with scents and think they help you, this will build your confidence and concentration, which will make you a better fisherman, whether the scent really works or not.

For smaller panfish, cut a fresh crawfish tail into several pieces and apply one to a small hook or jig dangled under a bobber.

LEECHES – Several kinds of leeches inhabit North American waters, but only ribbon leeches are widely used for bait. These leeches squirm actively when held; less desirable leeches are lifeless when held. Ribbon leeches are used primarily to catch walleye and bass.

To trap leeches, put dead minnows, liver, beef kidney or bones into a large coffee can and mash the top of the can almost shut. Sink the can in leech-infested waters overnight, and rapidly pull the can up the next morning. Leeches keep for a long time in a water-filled Styrofoam minnow bucket placed in the shade.

Leeches work well suspended under a bobber, since they squirm continuously. They may be trolled or crawled across bottom on a live-bait rig, slip-sinker rig or bottom-bouncer rig. They are also frequently used as a trailer on a lead-head jig. To hook a leech, run the point of the hook through the head.

CUT BAIT – Pieces or entrails of baitfish are excellent for catching catfish. Larger shad, herring, smelt and other oily baitfish are best. These can be netted, cut into chunks an inch square, and hooked onto bottom rigs. Since catfish are scent feeders, they home in on the oil and blood escaping from cut bait.

Also, a small slice of panfish meat adds to the attraction of a small jig for sunfish, white bass, crappie and yellow perch.

OTHER NATURAL BAITS – Baits listed above are the most popular natural baits, but they are not the only good ones. Many others are very effective on various fish species. Meal worms, wax worms, waterdogs, frogs, mayflies, salmon eggs, hellgrammites, grubs, catalpa

BASS PRO SHOPS
XPSLOCUST

BERKLEY FRENZY WALKER

EXCAL-ULTRALIGHT
GST MINNOW

ARBOGAST HULA POPPER

ARBOGAST
JITTERBUG

STRIKE KING
ELITE BUZZBAIT

worms, spring lizards and mussels are excellent baits for different species of fish.

Using Artificial Baits

Live worms and leeches wiggle on the hook. Live minnows swim. Live crawfish scoot across rocks or mud. But artificial baits hang motionless in the water until the angler gives them life by casting and retrieving. In most cases, the more skillfully this is done, the more fish a user will catch. This is why many anglers consider artificial baits more challenging than natural baits. You've got to add the life!

Following are short descriptions of various artificial lures and how to use them.

TOPWATERS – This is the oldest category of artificial baits and one of the best. Bass, muskies, pike, stripers, white bass, trout and other species feed on the surface, normally in warm months and low-light periods of early morning, late afternoon and night. Sometimes, though, fish will hit topwaters in the middle of a bright day. Basically, if you see surface-feeding activity, give topwaters a try.

Topwater baits include wood and plastic lures in a broad variety of shapes and actions.

Poppers (also called chuggers) have scooped-out heads which make slapping sounds when pulled with short, quick jerks.

Floating minnows rest motionless and then swim with a quiet, subtle side-to-side action when reeled in.

Stickbaits resemble cigars with hooks attached. They dart across the surface in a zig-zag pattern when pulled with short, quick snaps of the rod tip.

Crawlers have concave metal lips. This bait wobbles back and forth and makes popping noise on a steady retrieve.

Buzz baits have revolving metal or plastic blades that boil the water on a steady retrieve.

If fish are actively feeding on the surface, use a lure that works fast and makes a lot of noise. But if fish aren't active, select a quieter lure and work it slowly. (In this case, after the lure hits the water, let it sit still until all ripples disappear. Then twitch the lure slightly, and hold on!)

When casting a topwater lure, be ready for a strike when it hits the water. Sometimes fish see it coming through the air and take it immediately.

When a fish strikes a topwater lure, wait until the lure disappears

Plastic worms are among the most popular soft plastic lures, and are top producers of trophy bass. These lures are typically worked along bottom through stumps, brush, rocks and other cover where bass hang out.

underwater before setting the hook. This takes nerves of steel, since the natural tendency is to jerk the instant the strike occurs. However, a short delay will give the fish time to take the lure down and turn away with it, which increases your chance of getting a good hookset.

SPINNERS – This bait category includes spinnerbaits and in-line spinners. Spinnerbaits are shaped like an open safety pin. A rotating blade is attached to the upper arm; a leadhead body, skirt and hook are on the lower arm. This design makes a spinnerbait semi-weedless, so it can be worked through vegetation, brush, timber and stumps with few hang-ups.

Spinnerbaits come in a wide variety of sizes and blade configurations. Some have one blade, while others have two or more. Some have Colorado or Indiana blades (oval-shaped) for slower vibrations with more "thump," while others have willowleaf blades (elongated/ pointed) for faster, higher-pitched vibrations. Colorado/Indiana blades are better for slower retrieves for inactive fish. Willowleaf blades are made to retrieve faster (especially in current) and for fish that are actively chasing baitfish.

Spinnerbaits are normally associated with bass fishing, but they're also good on muskies and pike. Very small spinnerbaits can be effective on small panfish like crappie and sunfish.

The blade on an in-line spinner is attached to the same shaft as the body, and it revolves around it. Because of this compact design,

JOHNSON RATTLIN BEETLE

ABU GARCIA REFLEX SPINNER

BERKLEY SCENT VENT

STRIKE KING BLEEDING BAIT SPINNERBAIT

STRIKE KING COMPACT SILHOUETTE SPINNERBAIT

in-line spinners work well in current. These lures are typically used for smallmouth bass, rock bass, trout and other stream species.

Spinners are a good artificial lure for beginning anglers. In most cases, all you have to do is cast them out and reel them in. As your skills increase, you'll learn to vary retrieves and crawl spinnerbaits through cover or across bottom. In any case, when you feel a bump or see your line move sideways, set the hook immediately!

CRANKBAITS – This is another good lure family for beginners. Crankbaits are so-named because they have built-in actions. All you have to do is cast them and then crank the reel handle. The retrieve causes these baits to wiggle, dive and come to life.

Crankbaits are used mainly for largemouth and smallmouth bass, white bass, walleye, sauger, muskies and pike. They are effective in reservoirs, lakes and streams; around rocks, timber, docks, bridges, roadbeds and other structure. Generally they're not effective in vegetation, since their treble hooks foul in the weeds. However, crankbaits can be effective retrieved close to weeds or over the top of submerged vegetation.

Natural Bait and Artificial Lures 105

There are two sub-categories of crankbaits: "floater/divers," and "vibrating." Floater/divers usually have plastic or metal lips. They float on the surface at rest, but when the retrieve starts, they dive underwater and wiggle back and forth. Usually, the larger a bait's lip, the deeper it will run.

One of the secrets to success with floater/divers is to keep them bumping bottom or cover objects. To do this, you must retrieve them so they will dive as deeply as possible. Maximum depth may be achieved by (1) using smaller line (6-12 pound test is perfect), (2) cranking at a medium pace instead of too fast, (3) pointing your rod tip down toward the water during the retrieve, and (4) making long casts. Once the bait hits bottom, vary the retrieve speed or try sto-pand- go reeling to trigger strikes. Keep it working along bottom as long as possible before it swims back up to the rod tip. Sometimes a floater/diver crankbait gets "out-of-tune" and won't swim in a straight line. Instead, it veers off to one side or the other. To retune a lure, bend the eye (where you tie the line) in the direction opposite the way the lure is veering. Make small adjustments with a pair of

Diving crankbaits come in a broad range of sizes and designs. One of the secrets to success with diving crankbaits is to keep them digging along bottom. Anglers should learn how deep various crankbaits dive, then select one that best matches up with the water depth where they're fishing.

needlenose pliers, and test the lure's track after each adjustment to get it swimming straight.

Vibrating crankbaits are used in relatively shallow water where fish are actively feeding. These are sinking baits, so the retrieve must be started shortly after they hit the water. They should be reeled fast to simulate baitfish fleeing from a predator. This speed and tight wiggling action excites larger fish into striking.

SOFT PLASTICS – This family of baits includes plastic worms, grubs, minnows, tubes, lizards, crawfish, eels and other live bait imitations. These baits are natural-feeling and lifelike to fish. They are used mainly on bass, white bass, stripers, panfish, crappie, walleye and other species.

Soft plastics are very versatile lures. They can be fished without weight on the surface, or they can be weighted with a sinker or jighead and fished below the surface. They can be rigged weedless and fished through weeds, brush, rocks or stumps.

BILL LEWIS RAT-L-TRAP BLEEDING SHAD

BOMBER MODEL 8A

Plastic worms are among the most popular of soft plastic lures. The most common way to use them is to crawl or hop them along bottom structure. To do this, rig the worm according to the instructions under "Texas-Rigged Plastic Worms" in the previous chapter. Use a small slip sinker for fishing shallow water and a heavier sinker for deeper water. A good rule of thumb is to use a ⅛-ounce slip sinker in depths up to 6 feet; a ¼-ounce sinker from 6-12 feet; and a ⅜-½-ounce sinker in water deeper than 12 feet.

Cast the worm toward the structure and allow it to sink to the bottom. (You'll feel it hit or see your line go slack.) Hold your rod tip in the 10 o'clock position and reel up slack. Now quickly lift the rod tip to the 11 o'clock position without reeling. This lifts the worm off bottom and swims it forward a short distance. Then allow the worm to fall back to the bottom, reel up slack line, and repeat the process. This lift/drop/reel sequence should be repeated until the worm exits the main target area (tree top, brush, weedbed, etc.)

When hopping a plastic worm, be alert for any taps or bumps, and always watch your line for sudden, unnatural pulses or sideways movements. Sometimes strikes are obvious and easy to detect. Other times they are light and subtle. If you know you've got a bite, reel up slack line and set the hook immediately. But if you're not sure, reel up slack and hold the bait still for a few seconds. If nothing happens, tug on the bait ever so slightly. If you feel something tug back, set the hook!

To set the hook with a plastic worm, lower your rod tip to the 9 o'clock position, then set hard and fast with your wrists and forearms. If you don't feel that you have a good hookset, set again. This method applies to tackle spooled with line above 10-pound test. When you're using lighter line, set with less force, or you may break your line.

Virtually all soft plastic baits can be fished with the same lift/drop/reel technique described above. Also, grubs can be hopped along bottom or swum through mid-depth areas with a steady retrieve. Lizards and eels can be slithered through weeds and brush. Minnows can be threaded through sunken flats and timber. Crawfish can be bumped through rocks. Weightless worms and plastic stick

BERKLEY TOURNAMENT STRENGTH POWER JERK SHAD

BERKLEY MICRO POWER FROG

BERKLEY POWER LEECH

BERKLEY POWER TUBE

BERKLEY POWER CRAW

BERKLEY POWER LIZARD

lures can be worked over sunken vegetation and other cover. Experiment with various baits to see which the fish prefer.

JIGS – If there's such thing as a universal bait, the leadhead jig is it. These balls of lead with hooks running out the back can be used in a wide range of circumstances to catch almost all freshwater fish. Jigs are basic baits that all anglers should learn to use.

Jigs come in a wide range of sizes. Tiny jigs (1/32-ounce) will take trout or small panfish in shallow water. A 1-ounce jig might be used to bump bottom in heavy current for walleye or sauger. The most popular jig sizes are 1/16, 1/8 and 1/4-ounce.

Many veteran anglers keep different-size jigs in their tackle boxes and then select the right size for a particular fishing situation. This selection is based on the size of the target fish, depth of water, and amount of wind and current. The bigger the fish, the deeper the water, and the stronger the wind and current, the heavier the jig should be.

Jigs are almost always "dressed" with an artificial trailer or live bait. Some jigs are made with hair, feather or rubber skirts wrapped around the hook. Others come pre-rigged with plastic grubs. But the majority of jigs are sold without any trailer, leaving this choice up to the angler. You may install your own trailer (plastic grub, tube, small worm, pork rind), or you may prefer hooking on a live minnow, night crawler or leech. Also, in addition to trailers, some jigs have small spinners attached to the head of the lure to add flash.

There are several effective jig retrieves. The basic one is the lift/drop: allow the jig to sink to bottom, then hop it along bottom with short lifting jerks of the rod tip. (This is similar to the lift/drop/reel method for fishing a plastic worm, except faster.) Another popular

Soft plastic lures are effective on many types of fish. Soft plastics include worms, grubs, lizards, frogs and other natural bait imitations.

BOMBER FLAIR HAIR JIG

**STRIKE KING
BLEEDING BITSY BUG JIG**

**STRIKE KING
DENNY BRAUER PREMIER
PRO-MODEL JIG**

retrieve is the steady pull, swimming the jig in open water or just above bottom, sometimes grazing stumps, rocks or other structure.

A third retrieve is vertical jigging. Lower the jig straight down to bottom or into cover, lift it with the rod tip, then allow it to sink back down. Most strikes come when the bait is dropping.

As with plastic worms, strikes on jigs may be very hard or extremely light. An angler using a jig will usually feel a bump or "tick" as a fish sucks in the bait. The key to detecting this is keeping a tight line at all times. If you feel a bump or see unnatural movement, set the hook immediately. There's no waiting with jigs.

SPOONS – Metal spoons are the "old faithfuls" of artificial lures. They've been around a long time, and they're still producing. They are excellent for catching bass, walleye, pike, muskies and white bass.

Some spoons are designed to be fished on the surface, while others are for underwater use. In both cases, the standard retrieve is a slow, steady pull. Sometimes, however, an erratic stop/go retrieve may trigger more strikes.

Different baits serve specific purposes. Beginning anglers must learn what various baits are designed to do, then apply them where they work best. For instance, this jig/minnow combo is good for bumping along bottom for walleye, sauger, crappie and other panfish.

One special use for spoons is for fishing around or through weeds and surface-matted grass. Topwater spoons will ride over the thickest lily pads, moss, etc. Spoons retrieved underwater will flutter and dart through reeds and grass with minimal hang-ups. In this situation, a spoon with a weedguard over a single hook is recommended.

Trailers are frequently added to a spoon's hook for extra attraction. Pork strips or plastic or rubber skirts are standard trailers. When adding a skirt to a spoon's hook, run the hook's point through the skirt from back to front so the skirt will billow out during the retrieve.

COTTON CORDELL
GRAPPLER SHAD

LUHR-JENSEN RADAR 10

STRIKE KING
WILD SHINER
SUSPENDING JERK BAIT

JOHNSON SPRITE SPOON

Summary

In Chapter 4, I described rods, reels and line as "tools" for fishing. Baits are also tools in the truest sense. They are objects designed to help you catch fish. Different baits serve specific purposes. You must learn what various baits are designed to do, then apply them where they work best.

You start to do this by reading, but then you must apply what you read on the water. There's no better teacher than experience. Lakes and streams are your laboratory. This is where you'll carry out your experiments with various fishing tools.

Now you're ready to put the entire package together. You've learned about different fish species, where to fish, tackle, accessories, rigs, and now baits. We're finally ready to go fishing, to learn simple ways to catch fish from different types of waters. Let's move forward into what's probably the most important chapter in *Basic Fishing*.

Fishing is a lot more fun when you catch something, and catching fish means using the right bait or lure. Beginning anglers will learn through experience which baits/lures to use when, and how to do so properly.

CHAPTER 8

Basic Fishing Techniques

Before becoming an outdoor writer, I was a pilot in the U. S. Air Force, and I now realize that in an odd way, flying and fishing are alike. You can read books about flying for years, but before you climb into a cockpit, you don't know what flying is really like. Reading won't teach you how to take off, hold the wings straight and level, and land a plane. You have to get up in the clouds before you'll really get the feel of flying.

When fishing ponds and small lakes, anglers should concentrate on areas close to the bank, especially where there is some type cover (weeds, brush, logs, docks, etc.). They should keep moving and trying new areas until they learn where sunfish, bass, crappie and other species are holding.

The same is true about fishing. You can read about fishing, but you'll never be a fisherman until you put your book knowledge to practical use. This is where we'll get specific. This chapter will teach you practical, step-by-step techniques for taking fish from each of these spots.

In essence, then, this chapter is the heart of Basic Fishing. Now we'll talk mechanics of fishing, not theories. We'll cover exactly how to approach different situations. You've already learned about various species, how to find places to fish, select tackle and accessories, tie rigs and choose baits. This was all background material to prepare you for what's in this chapter, where we'll bind everything together.

Obviously it's impossible to cover all techniques for all fish. Instead, we'll look at the best opportunities and simplest techniques.

Also, I'll help you identify prime fishing locations in different types of waters, then tell you how to make them pay off.

Where Fish Live

The first step in catching fish is knowing where to find them. On each outing, regardless of where you go and what species you're after, you must first study your water to determine where fish are located.

Review the section in Chapter 1 entitled "Structure." This is the key in determining where fish are holding and where you can catch them. Remember that most fish gather in predictable places, and these places fall into what we call "structure."

A big catch like this largemouth bass comes through knowing where these fish live and which lure and techniques will get them to bite. In this chapter we'll talk specifics about how to catch fish from the broad variety of North American waters.

Various waters have different types of structure. In this chapter, I'll identify structure specific to ponds, lakes, streams and rivers and I'll explain how to fish them. First, you need to figure out where fish are most likely to be found. Then decide which combination of tackle, bait and method will be most effective in catching them.

You should go through this process each time you fish. First, location. Where should the fish be? Then, presentation. What's the best way to catch them? Follow this outline, and your fishing efforts will be orderly and successful instead of haphazard and ineffective.

How to Fish Ponds and Small Lakes

Farm ponds and small lakes are scattered throughout North America. They are the most numerous of all fishing waters and are some of the best fishing spots.

Some ponds are formed naturally by beavers, mud slides, etc. However, most ponds and small lakes are man made to provide water for livestock, irrigate fields and prevent erosion. Other ponds and small lakes were built strictly for recreation.

Small bodies of water are excellent places to learn to fish, for two reasons. First, many of them have abundant fish populations, but little fishing pressure, so the fish aren't spooky. And second, since these waters are small, the fish are more confined, so they're easier to locate. It doesn't take as long to test different locations and techniques. For this reason, I like to think of ponds and small lakes as "training grounds" to prepare you to fish more sophisticated waters.

A fallen tree or log can form an ideal hiding place for bass, sunfish, and other species. Be sure to carefully scout a small lake or pond for such underwater structure.

Analyzing Ponds and Small Lakes

When you get to a pond or small lake, your fishing starts before you wet a line. First you should study the pond to determine its characteristics. Some ponds have flat basins, while others have a shallow end with ditches running into it and a deep end with a dam. Many ponds have brush, weeds, trees, logs, rocks or other structure around the banks or in the water. Take note of all the combinations of depths and structure to determine which combination is holding the fish.

Again, consider your target species' basic nature. Where that fish will be located will vary according to the time of year and water conditions. For instance, bass might be in the shallows in spring and in deeper water in the summer. However, in the hottest months they might still feed in the shallows during night or at dawn and dusk. These are the types of things you must learn before you can make an educated guess about where to find fish.

Don't worry, you can learn the specifics of fish behavior as you go. For now, you can fish effectively if you follow the directions in the following section. These are basic, methods that produce fish consistently from one season and set of conditions to the next.

Techniques for Fishing Ponds and Small Lakes

Most ponds and small lakes support what biologists call "warm water fisheries:" sunfish, crappie, bass, catfish and bullheads. Some spring-fed ponds hold trout. Let's take these species one at a time and look specifically at how to catch them.

SUNFISH

Bluegill and other small sunfish are my choice for someone just starting out in fishing. These are usually the most plentiful fish in ponds and small lakes, and they always seem willing to bite.

In spring, early summer and fall, sunfish stay in shallow to medium-deep water (2-10 feet). In hottest summer and coldest winter, they normally move deeper, though they may still occasionally feed in the shallows.

Small sunfish love to hold around brush, logs, weeds, piers and other cover. On cloudy days or in dingy water, these fish often hang around edges of such structure. This is true during the early morning and late afternoon. But during the part of the day when the sun is brightest, especially in clear-water ponds, sunfish swim into brush or vegetation, under piers or tight to stumps and logs. On sunny days, they like to hide in shady areas.

If possible, get out early to fish for sunfish in a pond or small lake. Take a long panfish pole or light-action spinning or spin-cast rod and reel spooled with 4- or 6-pound test line. Tie a fixed-bobber rig with a longshank wire hook (#6 or #8), a little split shot, and a bobber. (Remember to balance the weight of your split shot and bobber!)

For bait, try earthworms, crickets or grasshoppers. Thread a small worm up the shank of the hook, or use only a small piece of nightcrawler. A whole cricket or grasshopper is the perfect-size bite for a bluegill.

Next, adjust the bobber so your bait hangs midway between the surface and the bottom. If you can't see bottom and you don't know how deep the pond is, begin fishing 2-4 feet deep. If you don't catch fish, experiment with other depths.

Let's say you think sunfish may be holding around weeds growing close to the bank. Drop your bait in next to the weeds. The bobber should be floating upright. If it's laying on its side, the bait is probably on bottom. In this case shorten the distance between the bobber and hook so the bait will suspend above the bottom.

Be careful not to stand right over the spot you're fishing, especially if

Ponds and small lakes are plentiful throughout North America, and many offer very good action on fish that rarely see baits or artificial lures. These diminutive waters are great places for beginners to learn the basics of this sport

the water's clear. The fish will see you and become spooky. Sometimes it's better to sit on the pond bank rather than stand. Wear natural-colored or camouflage clothing and avoid making any commotion that might scare the fish.

Sunfish will usually bite with little hesitation so if you don't get a bite in a couple of minutes, twitch your bait to get the fish's attention.

Carefully select locations to place your bait. Keep it close to cover, and if the fish aren't biting well, look for openings in cover where you can drop the bait without getting hung up.

If you're not getting bites, try something different. Fish around another type of structure. If you've been fishing in shallow water, try a deeper area. (Don't forget to lengthen the distance between your bobber and hook.) If the pond has a dam, drop your bait close to it. If there is an overflow, aerator or fish feeder, try around those.

Most anglers who pond-fish walk the banks, but you have two other options. You can fish from a small boat to cover more water, or you can wade-fish. This technique is especially good in ponds with a lot of brush, cattails or similar cover. In warm months, you can wadefish in old pants and tennis shoes.

Remember to "think structure." Don't drop your bait at some random spot in the middle of the pond and then sit and watch your bobber for an hour. Keep moving

One secret to fishing ponds and small lakes is to keep moving until you locate fish. A small boat will enable an angler to cover more water and prime fish locations.

until you begin catching fish. Then slow down and work the area thoroughly. Once you find a productive spot, stay with it as long as the fish keep biting.

A special opportunity exists during spring when sunfish are spawning. They fan nests in shallow water (2-5 feet deep) around the banks and especially in the shallow end of a pond. Often you can see the nests. They're about the size of a dinner plate, and they appear light against the dark pond bottom. Usually, many nests will be clustered in the same area.

When you see these "beds," set your bobber shallow and drop your bait right next to them, trying not to spook the fish. You're probably better off casting into the beds rather than sneaking in close with a long pole.

CRAPPIE

Fishing for crappie in ponds and small lakes is similar to fishing for bluegill and sunfish. Always fish close to structure and stay on the move until you find fish. The primary difference is the bait you use. Crappie prefer minnows over other natural baits, and they readily attack small jigs and spinners.

Long poles are a favorite with crappie fishermen. Many crappie experts quietly skull a small boat from one piece of structure to the

Little waters can yield some big catches like the lunker bass at right. A good way to go after bass in ponds and small lakes to wadefish. Wading allows you to slip up close to bass hiding spots and present a bait in just the right location.

next, and use a panfish pole to dangle a float rig with a minnow or jig in next to cover. They ease their bait down beside a tree or piece of brush, leave it for a moment, pick it up, set it down on the other side, then move to the next spot. In small lakes and ponds, crappie scatter throughout the shallow structure, and this "hunt-andpeck" method of fishing is very effective. This is especially true in spring, when the fish move into shallow cover to spawn. You can also use this method while wade-fishing or fishing from shore, if the structure is within reach.

Another good crappie technique is to use a slip-bobber rig with a spinning or spin-cast outfit. Hook a live minnow through the back onto a thin wire hook (#2) or through the lips on a lightweight (1/16 or 1/32 ounce) jig. Then cast this rig next to a weedline, brush-pile or log

If you don't get a bite in 5 minutes, try somewhere else. If you get a bite, don't yank if the bobber is just twitching. Wait for the bobber to start moving off or disappear beneath the surface before setting the hook. Crappie have soft mouths, so don't set too hard, or you'll rip out the hook. Instead, lift up on your pole or rod, and you should have the fish.

If you don't catch fish shallow, try deeper water, especially during hot summer months or on bright, clear days. Adjust your bobber up the line and drop your bait right in front of the dam or off the end of a pier. Try casting into the middle of the pond and see what happens. With this method of fishing, 6- 10 feet is not too deep. There is less certainty in this technique, however, because you're hunting for crappie in a random area.

To cover a lot of water, cast a 1/16-ounce jig or a small in-line spinner. After casting, count slowly as the bait sinks. After a few seconds, begin your retrieve. Try different counts (depths). If you get a bite, let the bait sink to the same count next time. You may have found the depth where crappie are holding. This technique is called the "countdown" method of fishing with a sinking bait.

When retrieving the jig, move it at a slow to moderate pace, and alternate between a straight pull and a rising/falling path back through the water. With the spinner, a slow, straight retrieve is best. Crappie will usually bite if you pull either of these baits past them.

A spinnerbait is a super-productive lure for catching bass in ponds and small lakes. This is an easy lure to use. Simply cast it and reel back with a steady, medium-paced retrieve. Most strikes come around cover where bass hide to watch for prey.

BASS

Bass fishing is more complicated than fishing for sunfish or crappie, partly because of all the different types of bass tackle and lures. Bass are still members of the sunfish family, however, and they share certain behavior characteristics with bluegill and crappie. Anywhere you're likely to catch these latter fish, you're apt to find bass, since they all hold around the same types of structure.

Let's begin with the simplest technique. You can catch bass on a long cane or fiberglass pole, but you need a stronger pole than you used on bluegill, and your line should be at least 12- pound test.

Tie on a slip-bobber rig with the bobber set at around 3 feet. Use a 1/0 or 2/0 steel hook. Add a light sinker 6 inches up from the hook. Then bait this rig with a gob of nightcrawlers or a live minnow hooked through the back.

Drop your line near likely fish-holding spots, but don't leave it in one place for more than 2-3 minutes. If a bass is there, it'll usually take the bait. When you get a bite, wait for the bobber to disappear before setting the hook. Then pull the fish quickly to the surface and land it.

When using the long-pole method, work your way around the pond, being careful not to let the fish see you. They are skittish when they're in shallow water, and they'll spook easily.

While this long-pole method is a good one, most experienced fishermen go after pond bass with casting or spinning tackle and artificial lures. Casting allows you to reach targets farther away and also to cover more water. Many artificial lures will catch pond bass, but my three favorites are topwaters, spinnerbaits and plastic worms.

Try topwaters early in the morning, late in the afternoon or at night (during summer). Use topwaters when the sky is overcast, especially when the surface is calm. In warmer months, I prefer poppers and propeller baits that make a lot of noise and attract bass from a distance. In early spring, I like a quieter floating minnow.

Cast topwaters close to weeds, beside logs, along dams or anywhere you think bass might be holding. Cast past a particular object, then work the bait up to where you think the fish are. Allow the bait to rest motionless for several seconds, then twitch it just enough to cause the slightest ripple on the water. This is usually when the strike comes!

If a spot looks good, but you don't get a strike, cast back to it several times. Sometimes when bass are "inactive" (aren't feeding), you have to arouse their curiosity or agitate them into striking, and repeat casts may do this.

At times, though, bass just won't strike a surface lure. If you don't get any action on a topwater lure in 15 minutes, switch to a spinnerbait and try the same area. Keep your retrieve steady, and try different speeds (fast, medium, slow). You might try try "fluttering" the bait - allowing it to sink momentarily after it runs past a log, treetop or other cover. This can trigger a strike from a bass that's following the lure during a steady retrieve.

Don't be afraid to retrieve a spinnerbait through brush and weeds. If you keep reeling while it coming through cover, this lure is virtually weedless. You may hang occasionally (use strong line with these baits so you can pull them free), but you'll get more strikes by fishing the thick stuff.

Plastic worms are what I call "last resort baits." Bass can usually be coaxed into striking worms when they won't hit other lures, and plastic worms can be worked slower and through the thickest cover. They're also good for taking bass in deep water. Plastic worms are top prospects for mid-day fishing in hot weather.

For pond bass, use a 4-7½-inch plastic worm rigged Texas-style with a ¹⁄₁₆-¼ oz. sliding sinker. (The heavier sinker is for deeper water.) Cast it right into cover or close to it. (Make sure the point of the hook is embedded inside the worm.) Then crawl it slowly through the cover, lifting it with

A variety of lures can be used to catch stream bass and smaller panfish. Spinners, diving crankbaits, topwater minnows and plastic worms and tubes are all deadly on fish that inhabit small moving waters.

the rod tip, then allowing it to settle back to the bottom.

When fishing lily pads, brush or other thick vegetation, cast to openings and pockets. Cast off points, ends of weedbeds or riprap, and corners of piers. These are places where bass are likely to hang.

If you don't get action in the shallows, and you suspect the bass are deeper, it's time to change tactics. Since you can't see underwater, you must locate structure by interpreting what you can from the surface. Find a gully feeding into the shallow end of the pond. Then try to imagine how this gully runs along the pond bottom, and cast your plastic worm along it. This can be prime bass-holding structure.

A second deep-water strategy is to cast a plastic worm into the deep end or along the dam, then crawl it back up the bank. The third option is to simply walk along the bank and cast at random, hoping you'll locate bass along some unknown structure under the water. In all cases, however, it's very important to allow your plastic worm to sink to bottom before starting your retrieve. When casting to deep spots, if you get a bite or catch a fish, cast back to that same spot several more times. Bass often school together in deep water.

There are other baits you might use in special situations. Many ponds have heavy weedbeds or lily pads. You can fish them with a topwater spoon that wobbles over plants and attracts bass lying underneath. Leadhead jigs tipped with a plastic trailer (grub, crawfish, etc.) can be hopped across bottom when searching deep-water areas. Diving crankbaits are good for random casting into deep spots.

CATFISH/BULLHEADS

Catfish and bullheads spend the most time on or near the bottom of small ponds and lakes, so this is where you should fish for them. While they prefer deep water, they may move up and feed in the shallows from time to time. In either location, fish directly on bottom without a float or just above bottom with a float.

While you move a lot searching for sunfish, crappie and bass, fishing for catfish and bullheads calls for a pick-one-spot-and-wait-'em-out method. These fish find their food mostly by smell and you have to leave your bait in one place long enough for the scent to spread through the water and for the fish to home in on it.

It's possible to fish for these species with long poles, but I prefer

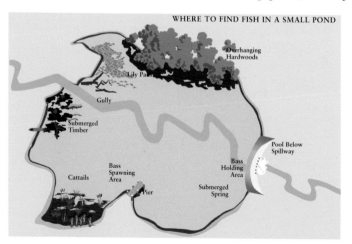

WHERE TO FIND FISH IN A SMALL POND

Overhanging Hardwoods

Lily Pads

Gully

Submerged Timber

Cattails

Bass Spawning Area

Pier

Submerged Spring

Bass Holding Area

Pool Below Spillway

Carefully examine small ponds for features that provide fish holding areas. The map above shows typical features encountered in a farm pond, such as sunken timber and brush piles, shallow weed beds, and a submerged creek channel

spin-cast or spinning outfits so I can fish farther off the bank. I take at least two rods. I pick a spot on the bank close to deep water. Then I cut a forked stick for each rod and push it into the ground next to the pond's edge. I cast out my lines, prop my rods in the forked sticks, and wait for something to happen.

When using two rods, I tie a bottom rig on one and a slip-bobber rig on the other. This gives the catfish or bullheads a choice of a bait laying on bottom or hanging just above.

Catfish grow much larger than bullheads, so if catfish are your main target, you need larger hooks. I recommend a #1 or 1/0 sproat or baitholder hook. If you're fishing for bullheads, select a smaller #6 hook. If you're trying for both species, use something in between – a #2 or #4.

Catfish and bullheads will eat the same baits. Earthworms or nightcrawlers are two favorites. Chicken liver, live or dead minnows, grasshoppers and a wide variety of commercially-made baits also work well. With all these baits, load your hooks. The more bait on them, the more scent you have in the water, and the more likely you are to attract fish.

Cast your baited lines into deep water. With the bottom rig, wait until the sinker is on bottom, then gently reel in line until all the slack is out. With a slip-bobber rig, set the bobber so the bait is suspended just above bottom.

Now, just relax and wait. When a fish takes the bottom-rig bait, the rod tip will jump. When there's a bite on the slip-bobber bait, the bobber will dance nervously on the surface.

If you get a bite, don't set the hook until the fish starts swimming away with the bait. Pick up the rod and get ready to set the hook, but don't exert any pull until the line starts moving steadily off or the bobber goes under and stays. Then strike back hard and begin playing your fish.

If you're not getting bites, how long do you stay in one place before moving to another? Probably the best answer is "as long as you can stand it." The best catfishermen are usually the ones with the most patience. But at a minimum, you should fish in one spot at least 20 minutes before moving somewhere else.

Catfish like to feed in lowlight periods of dawn, dusk or night. For night fishing, buy a small metal

A boat is a definite help in fishing a large lake or reservoir. Anglers who can move around and fish away from the bank have a better chance of success on these larger waters.

bell and fasten it to the end of your rod. When you get a bite, the bell will ring, indicating that a fish has your bait.

TROUT

Trout are generally thought of as fish of streams and large lakes. However, they can also live in cool-water ponds. Northern beaver ponds are great places for wild brook trout, and spring-fed manmade ponds can sustain stocked rainbows.

Trout do not relate to structure the way warm-water fish do. They roam a pond or small lake and are likely to be found at any depth. The best way to find them is to walk the bank and try different areas. You can catch trout on either natural bait or artificials. Use spin-cast or spinning tackle and 4- or 6-pound test line. For fishing natural bait, you can use either a bobber rig or a very light slip-sinker rig. Bait with a night crawler, grasshopper, commercially preserved salmon eggs, or whole kernel corn. Use a #8 short-shank hook.

If you prefer artificials, stick with tiny crankbaits, sinking spoons, in-line spinners (probably best), and minnow lures. If you're casting a lure that sinks, use the countdown method to fish different depths.

How to Fish Large Lakes and Reservoirs

Large lakes and reservoirs are some of the most popular and accessible fishing locations. Most are public waters with boat ramps, piers and other facilities to accommodate fishermen. They usually have large, diverse fish populations, and offer many opportunities for anglers.

What's the difference between a lake and a reservoir? A lake is made by nature, while a reservoir is made by man. Natural lakes are plentiful in the northern U. S. and Canada, in Florida, along major river systems (oxbows), and in the Western mountains.

Natural lakes come in several forms. Some have rounded, shallow basins with soft bottoms. Others are very deep with irregular shapes and bottoms that include reefs, islands and other structure. In many natural lakes, vegetation grows abundantly in shallow areas.

Natural lakes vary in age and fertility – measures of their ability to support fish populations. Some are relatively young and fertile, while others are eons old and somewhat infertile.

Reservoirs exist throughout North America. These are impoundments formed by building a dam across a river and backing up the floodwaters. Dozens of reservoirs have been built across the continent in the last 50 years to control floods, and generate electric power.

In most cases, the bottoms of reservoirs were once farmlands or forest. The water covers old fields, woodlands, creeks, roads, and other features that, when submerged, became structure.

Reservoirs are divided into two categories: upland and lowland (or mainstream). Upland reservoirs were built in highlands or canyons. They

Ethics & Etiquette

Ask First.
Don't trespass. Never go on private property without permission. If you find a place you'd like to fish, seek out the permission of the landowner

are typically deep and wind through steep terrain. Their coves and creek arms are irregular in shape.

In contrast, lowland reservoirs course through broad, flat valleys. These reservoirs are wider and shallower than upland reservoirs and typically have a long, fairly straight trunk with numerous smaller tributary bays.

The fertility of a reservoir often depends on how fertile the area was before it was flooded. Lowland reservoirs impounded over river bottoms are highly fertile, especially if trees were left standing when the area was flooded. As the trees decay, they release nutrients that support fish. Upland or canyon areas are less fertile, however. This is why upland reservoirs seldom support fish populations as dense as those in lowland reservoirs.

Analyzing Large Lakes and Reservoirs

It's easy for a beginning angler to stand on the bank of a large lake or reservoir and feel overwhelmed. There's so much water and so many places where fish can be. Start by adjusting your attitude. Since there's more water, there are more fish, so your odds of success are roughly the same as when fishing a pond or smaller lake.

Bluegill are favorite targets for many pond fishermen. These fish are aggressive biters, hard fighters and delicious to eat. Most bluegill are caught on live bait presented with a float rig around shady structure.

That's exactly how to approach this situation! It's impossible to fish an entire large lake or reservoir. So choose one small part of it, approach it like a pond or small lake, and use the same tactics. Whether they live in large or small waters, fish react the same to similar conditions in their environment. The basics still apply, and the same tactics work in large waters and small. The main difference is that, since they aren't confined in small ponds, the fish have more freedom to roam, and may migrate from one area to another depending on the season, food supply and other factors. Therefore, when deciding where to fish on a big lake, you have to pick the right small part.

How do you do this? Ask a nearby tackle store operator where the fish are biting. Watch where other anglers are fishing. Try to determine if the fish are shallow or deep. Learn the depth where they're biting. Use whatever information you can to get an overall picture then key in on a location.

One aid that all anglers should learn to use is a topographic map. A "topo" map shows water depth and contour changes on the lake bottom. You can look at a topo map and find drop-offs, reefs, flats, creek channels, sunken islands and other types of structure. You can use the map to find these special areas where fish are likely to hang out. For instance, if a tackle store operator tells you crappie are spawning around the shoreline in shallow bays, you can locate shallow bays on your topo map, learn how to get to there, then go fish them.

In essence, topo maps are road maps to hot spots. Get one for the lake where you plan to fish and begin studying it.

Techniques for Fishing Large Lakes and Reservoirs

Again, large lakes and reservoirs support many different fish species. Some have only warm-water fish, some only cold-water fish, and others a mix of the two. When you go fishing, single out which species you'd like to catch, then tailor your efforts to it.

Obviously, it's impossible to discuss all places and methods for catching different types of fish from large lakes and reservoirs. Instead, following are the best, easiest big-water opportunities for beginning anglers. I'll identify key areas and times, then I'll explain how to fish them.

SUNFISH

There's little difference in fishing for sunfish in small ponds or in large lakes. Catching them is a simple matter of figuring out their locations and then getting a bait in front of them.

In spring, sunfish migrate into shallow areas to spawn, so look for them in bays and pockets along wind-protected shorelines. Before spawning, sunfish hold around brush, stumps, weeds, rocks or other structure in 2-8 feet of water. Then, as the water temperature climbs into the mid-60° F range, sunfish will move up into 1-4 feet of water and spawn in areas that have firm bottoms – gravel, sand, clay.

Long poles or light-action spinning or spin-cast tackle will take these fish. Use fixed or slip-bobber rigs with wiggler worms, crickets or a small hair jig tipped with a maggot for bait. When fishing around cover, keep your bait close in. When fishing a spawning area, drop the bait right into the beds. (When fishing a visible sunfish spawning bed, try the outer edge first, then work your way to the center. This keeps fish that are hooked and struggling from spooking other fish off their beds.)

If it's spawning time and no beds are visible, fish through likely areas and keep moving until you start getting bites. If sunfish are around, they'll bite with little hesitation, so don't stay very long in one place if you're not getting any action.

After spawning, sunfish head back to deeper water. Many fish will still hold around visible cover, but they prefer to be near deep water. Two classic examples are a weedline on the edge of a drop-off and a steep rocky bank.

Besides a bobber rig, another good way to take sunfish is "jump-jigging," which involves casting a 1/16-ounce tube jig around weeds or rocks. Use a very light spinning outfit. Slowly reel the tube jig away from the cover and let the jig sink along the edge. Set the hook when you feel a bump or tug. This technique requires a boat, since you have to be over deep, open water casting into the weeds.

Docks, fishing piers and bridges are good locations to catch post-spawn sunfish. The water may be deep, but usually the fish will be up near the surface, holding under or close to the structures. Don't stand on a dock, pier or bridge and cast far out into the water. The fish are likely to be under your feet! Set your bobber so your bait hangs deeper than you can see, then keep your bait close to the structure.

Sometimes you have to experiment with different depths to find where sunfish are holding, and you should change location if you're not getting bites. Once you find the fish, work the area thoroughly. Sunfish swim in big schools after spawning, and you can catch several in one place.

One special sunfish opportunity exists when insects are hatching. If you can find insects swarming over the water and fish swirling beneath them, get ready for some hot action! Just thread one of the flies onto a small hook, and drop it into this natural dining room.

CRAPPIE

Crappie follow the same seasonal patterns as sunfish, except slightly earlier. When spring breaks, crappie head into bays and quiet coves to get ready to spawn. When the water warms into the low-60° F range, they fan out into the shallows. They spawn in or around brush, reeds, stumps, logs, roots, submerged timber, artificial fish attractors or other cover. Crappie spawning depth depends on water color. In dingy water, they may spawn only a foot or two deep. But in clear water, they'll spawn deeper, as far down as 12 feet. A good depth to try is 1 to 2 feet below the depth at which your bait sinks out of sight.

Minnows or small plastic jigs are good baits to try. Drop them next to or into potential spawning cover. You can do this from the bank, from a boat, or by wade-fishing the shallows. Lower the bait, wait 30 seconds, then move the bait to another spot. When fishing a brush pile, treetop or reed patch, try moving the bait around in the cover. If you catch a fish, put the bait back into the same spot to try for another. Stay on the move until you find some action.

After crappie spawn, they head back toward deeper water, where they collect along underwater ledges, creek channel banks and other sharp bottom contour breaks. This is where a topo map can help. If you're fishing from shore, look for spots where deep water runs close to the bank.

Then go to these areas and look for treetops, brush, logs or other visible cover. Fish these spots with minnows or jigs. Or, if there is no visible cover, cast jigs randomly from shore. Wait until the jig sinks to the bottom before starting your retrieve. Then use a slow, steady retrieve to work the bait back up the bank. Set the hook when you feel any slight "thump" or when you see your line twitch.

Fish attractors are another good crappie opportunity. Many fish and wildlife agencies sink brush or other cover into prime deep-water areas to concentrate fish. These attractors are then marked so anglers can find them. They may be out in a bay or around fishing piers or bridges. Dangle minnows or jigs around and into the middle of the cover. You'll hang up once in awhile, but you'll also catch fish.

Fall may be the second best time to catch crappie in large lakes and reservoirs. When the water starts cooling, they move back

Don't let the size of a lake or reservoir intimidate you. Fish do the same things in big lakes that they do in small ponds. Bass, bluegill and others often hang around rocky banks.

into shallow areas, holding around cover. Troll slowly through bays, casting jigs or dropping minnows into likely spots.

BASS

Spring, early summer and fall are the three best times for beginning anglers to try for bass. This is when the fish are aggressive and shallow. When they're deep, they may be tough even for the pro's to find.

During these seasons, bass spend most of their time in or near cover like brush, weeds, lily pads, flooded timber, logs, docks, stumps, rocks, riprap and bridge pilings. By casting around such structure, you've always got a chance for a strike.

In spring, bass spawn in shallow, wind-sheltered coves and shorelines, especially the ones with hard bottoms of sand, gravel or clay. During the spawning season, try topwater minnows, spinnerbaits and plastic lizards in these areas. Bass love to locate their nests next to features that offer protection from egg-eating sunfish.

After spawning, bass may stay shallow for several weeks. This is a good time to fish points – ridges of land that run off into the water.

Stand on the tip of a point and fan-cast crankbaits, plastic worms or splashy topwater lures (poppers, prop baits) around the point. Pay special attention to any structure – brush, stumps, rocks or weeds. If you don't get a strike the first time through such a high-potential spot, cast back to it. Sometimes you have to goad bass into striking.

Despite the warm water temperatures of summer, good bass fishing can still be found. Try fishing early and late in the day. Some bass will feed in the shallows during these low-light periods, then retreat to deeper water during mid-day. Other bass will hold along deeper areas or on the edges of shallow flats that border deeper water. Work your way along reefs, weedlines, channel drop-offs, edges of standing timber, sunken road-beds or even around boat docks. Also, cast to any isolated piece of cover, such as a log, brush top or rock pile.

Crankbaits and spinnerbaits are good lures for hot-weather bass, since you can fish them fast and cover a lot of water. If you go through a likely area without getting a bite, work back through it with a Texas-rigged plastic worm. Move around and try to find where fish are concentrated. In the warm months, this will typically be where a food supply – usually minnows – is available. If you can find baitfish, bass will be close by.

In fall, concentrate on shorelines and shallows in coves. Water temperature cools off in these areas first, and this cool-down draws in

Big bass and catfish will sometimes lurk in hollows in a pond or river bank formed by erosion beneath fallen trees. Catfish favor these "holes" during spawning season.

both baitfish and bass. Use the same tactics and baits you did in spring. Pay special attention to cover spots and the presence of minnows. If you see schools of minnows and bigger fish working around them, cast to these areas with a lipless crankbait in a shad color. In reservoirs try the extreme backs of major bays, where feeder creeks empty into the reservoir.

CATFISH/BULLHEADS

Big lakes can hold big catfish, and the best time to catch them is in late spring during the spawn. These fish move to the banks and look for holes and protected areas to lay their eggs.

Look for banks with big rock bluffs, riprap, etc. Catfish like to spawn in rocks. Fish around these areas with fixed or slip-bobber rigs baited with gobs of wiggler worms or night crawlers. Set your float so the bait hangs just above the rocks. Use medium strength line (10-20 pound test) and a steel hook (#1-3/0), since the possibility of hooking a big fish is good.

After they spawn, catfish head back to deepwater flats and channels. Normally they spend daylight hours deep, and move up at night to feed in nearby shallows. Find a point or other spot where the bank slopes off into deep water, and fish here from late afternoon well into the night. Use a bottom rig, baited with worms, cut bait, liver, commercial stink bait, or other popular catfish baits.

Another easy and productive method for taking catfish is called "jug fishing." This method requires a boat and 25 or more milk or 2-liter soft drink plastic bottles. Tie strong lines of 4-6 feet onto the jug handles or around the spouts. Tie a 2/0 steel hook on the end of the line, and add a split shot or a clincher sinker 6 inches

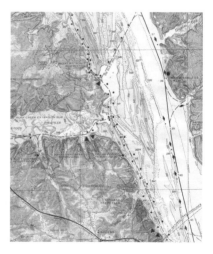

U.S. Geological Survey (USGS) topographical maps, such as the one shown above, provide detailed information about the bottom features and shorelines of lakes, rivers and impoundments.

up from the hook. Bait these lines with minnows, fish guts, or other catfish bait, and throw the jugs overboard on the upwind side of a lake or bay. The wind will float the jugs across the water, and catfish will be drawn to the bait. When a jug starts bobbing on the surface, move the boat in and retrieve the fish.

Bullheads normally stay in warm bays that have silty or muddy bottoms. Like catfish, they hold deep during the day, but move up shallow and feed from late afternoon through the night.

The technique for catching bullheads is the same as for night-feeding catfish, except you need lighter tackle. A spinning rod, 6-pound test line and a #3 hook are a good combination. A small split shot should be clamped on the line a foot up from the hook. Worms are good bait for bullheads.

WALLEYE

Walleye are traditionally deep-water, bottom-hugging fish, but they will frequently feed in the shallows. The determining factor seems to be light penetration into the water. Walleye don't like bright sunlight. But on overcast days, at night, when shallow areas are dingy or wave-swept, or when heavy weed growth provides shade, they may hold and feed in water no deeper than a couple of feet.

Walleye may be the ultimate structure fish. In deep areas, they hold along underwater humps, reefs and drop-offs on hard, clean bottoms, especially those with rock or sand. They prefer water with good circulation and rarely concentrate in dead-water areas like sheltered bays or coves. Walleye will move in and out of feeding areas.

Walleye spawn when water temperature climbs into the mid-40° F range, and this is a good time for beginning anglers to try for these fish. (Check local regulations, some states maintain a closed season on walleye until after they spawn.)

Look for shallows or shoal areas with gravel or rock bottoms that are exposed to the wind. Sloping points, islands, reefs, and rock piles close to shore are high-percentage spots. Fish them during lowlight periods – dawn, dusk and at night.

Try a slip-bobber rig baited with a night crawler, leech or live minnow in these areas. Adjust the bobber so the bait is suspended just above

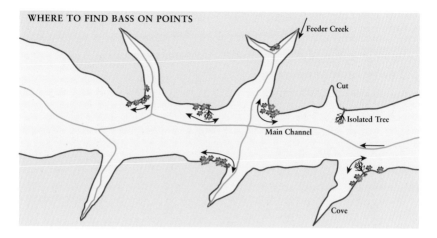

WHERE TO FIND BASS ON POINTS

Feeder Creek

Cut

Isolated Tree

Main Channel

Cove

Large rivers are among the most diverse of North America's waters. Big rivers have a broad range of fish and structure where fish concentrate. Look for bass, after spawning, off points that lead into submerged feeder creek channels.

bottom. Try casting shallow areas with jigs tipped with live minnows or shallow-running crankbaits.

In early summer, walleye can be caught along weedlines and mid-lake structure, both requiring a boat to properly fish them. When fishing weeds, cast a small jig (1/16 or 1/8 ounce) tipped with a minnow right into the edge of the weeds, then swim it back out. Work slowly along the weedline. Pay special attention to sharp bends in the weedline or areas where the weeds thin out. (This technique will also produce bass, crappie and pike.)

Fishing deep structure can be a needle in a haystack situation, so it's best to stay on the move until you locate fish. If you see other boats clustered on a small area, they're probably fishing productive structure. Go there and try drifting a night crawler on a slip-sinker rig. Move upwind of the other boats, and let out enough line to hit bottom. Then engage your reel and drag the night crawler across bottom as you drift downwind.

A bite will feel like a light tap or bump. Release line immediately, and allow the fish to swim off with the bait. After about 20 seconds, reel up slack, feel for the fish, and set the hook.

This is the standard way to fish for lake or reservoir walleye, but there are other good methods.

Bottom-bouncing rigs trailing night crawlers or minnows can be productive along deep structure or submerged points. This is the same principle as using the slip-sinker rig. Let your line down to bottom, engage the reel, then drag the rig behind you as you drift or troll. A slip-bobber rig drifted across this structure is also a good bet.

As you fish deep structure, it's a good idea to have a floating marker handy. If you get a bite, throw out the marker, then come back to this spot after you've landed your fish. Walleye are school fish, so there are probably more in the same area.

Beginners should try two other simple approaches for walleye. First, find a rocky shoreline that slopes off quickly into deep water. Fish this from dusk to around midnight, either with live bait (slip-bobber

rig) or by casting floating minnow lures. Second, cast into areas where strong winds are pushing waves into shore. This wave action muddies the water and walleye move right up to the banks to feed. Cast a jig and minnow into this roily water. Either walk the bank or wade the shallows, casting as you go. Pay special attention to the zone where muddy water borders clear.

WHITE BASS

White bass are open water fish. During spring spawning season, they migrate up tributaries but, at other times, they are usually in the main body of a lake or reservoir, schooled up to feed on small baitfish.

The best chance for beginners to catch white bass occurs when they're surface feeding. From early summer through fall, schools of

Trophy walleye like this one can be caught from many of North America's big lakes and reservoirs. These fish usually stay in deeper water and hug bottom structure. Sometimes, though, when feeding and water conditions are just right, they will move up into shallow vegetation or close to shore.

white bass herd baitfish to the surface and then slash through them, feeding savagely. This typically happens in reservoirs when water is being pulled through the dam to generate electricity. Resulting current concentrates shad minnows where they are vulnerable to white bass. Baitfish try to escape by heading to the surface. When white bass are feeding "in the jumps," almost any bright, fast-moving lure cast into this action will get a strike.

White bass normally feed around sunken islands, reefs, flats near the main channel, or where submerged creeks empty into the main channel. Usually white bass will surface feed for a short period, go back down to wait for another school of baitfish, then feed again. Hang around known surface feeding areas, and then cast fast and furiously when the fish appear.

NORTHERN PIKE

Pike fishing is best in spring, early summer and fall, when these fish are in quiet, weedy waters. They are normally aggressive, attacking any moving target. Look for pike in bays, sloughs, flats and coves that

Big catfish can be caught from large rivers by anglers who learn the right techniques. Heavy tackle and natural bait are the standard presentation. Rivers can produce catfish as large as 100 pounds.

have submerged weedbeds, logs or other "hideout" structure. Pike like fairly shallow water—3-10 feet.

Pike can get big, and even small ones are tough fighters, so use fairly heavy tackle. (Use 12-20 pound line.) They have sharp teeth that can easily cut monofilament. For this reason, always rig with a short steel leader ahead of your lure or bait.

Find a place that gives you access to likely cover. Cast a large, brightly-colored spoon next to or over this cover. You can cast from the bank or wade-fish, staying on the move to cover a lot of water. If you have a boat, motor to the upwind side of a shallow bay and drift slowly downwind, casting to clumps of weeds and weed edges. Retrieve the spoon steadily, but if pike don't seem interested, pump the spoon up and down or jerk it erratically to get their attention. Other good lures for pike are large spinnerbaits, in-line spinners, large floating minnows, and wide-wobbling crankbaits.

Live-bait fishing is extremely effective. A large minnow suspended under a fixed-bobber rig is almost irresistible to Pike. Clip a strong 1/0 or 2/0 hook to the end of a wire leader. Add a couple of split shot above the leader. Then add a large round bobber at a depth so the minnow will be up off bottom. Hook the minnow in the lips or back.

Cast this rig to weedlines, pockets, points or other structure. Then sit back and wait for a bite. When the bobber goes under, give the fish slack as it makes its first run with the bait. When the pike stops, reel in slack line, feel for the fish, and set the hook hard!

YELLOW PERCH

Yellow perch spawn in early spring when the water temperature climbs into the high 40° F range. They head into a lake's feeder streams or shallows, and during this migration, they are extremely easy to catch.

A fixed- or slip-bobber rig is a good choice for perch. Use light line (4-8 pound test) and a #6 long-shank hook. Add a small split shot and bobber, bait with worms or live minnows, and drop the bait into shallow areas around cover. If you don't get quick action, try somewhere else.

After the spawn, these fish return to main lake areas. Smaller fish hold along weedlines, and jump-jigging is a good way to take them. (Refer to the "Sunfish" part of this section.) Larger perch move

Since they're not subjected to much fishing pressure, stream fish like this smallmouth bass are more likely to bite a lure that's pulled past where they're holding.

onto reefs, ledges and deep points, and hang close to bottom. They may hold as deep as 40 feet.

Again, ask bait dealers about good deep-water perch spots. When you find one, fish it with a twohook panfish rig. Bump your bait along bottom to attract strikes. If you catch a fish, unhook it quickly and drop a fresh bait right back into the same spot. Other perch will be drawn by the commotion.

How to Fish Small Streams

Large lakes and reservoirs may be North America's most popular fishing spots, but streams are surely the most overlooked. Fish-filled streams flow throughout the continent, yet most receive only a fraction of the fishing pressure that big lakes do. This means that stream fish are oftentimes naïve and therefore easier to catch.

Streams can be divided into two classifications: warm- and cold-water. Warm-water streams harbor typical warm-water species: bass, sunfish, catfish, white bass. They range in character from clear, fast-moving, whitewater-and-rock streams to muddy, slow, deep streams.

Cold-water streams are normally found at higher altitudes or in valleys that drain highlands. Their primary gamefish are various trout species.

Cold-water streams are usually clean and fairly shallow, and they have medium-to-fast current. Their bottoms are typically rock, gravel or sand. You can fish small streams by any of three methods: bank-fishing, wading or floating.

When wade-fishing, you should work upstream, since you'll continually stir up silt and debris. By fishing upcurrent sediment drifts behind you instead of in front of you, so the fish aren't alerted to your presence.

Floating takes more planning and effort than wading, but it may also offer greater rewards. On many streams, floating can take you into semi-virgin fishing territory. I prefer a canoe when float-fishing, but johnboats and inflatables also work.

Analyzing Small Streams

Current is the primary influence in the life of a stream. It is like "liquid wind," blowing food downstream and shaping the environment. Current determines where fish will find food and cover and is why stream fishermen must always be aware of current and how it affects fish location.

Basically, fish react to current in one of three ways. One, they may be out in the fast water chasing food. Two, they might position themselves in an eddy right at the edge of current where they can watch for food without using much energy. And three, they will locate in quiet pools where current is slow. Different species vary in the amount of current they prefer and the places they hold.

The typical stream is made up of a series of shallow riffles where current is swift; deep pools where current is slow; and medium-depth runs where current is intermediate. Riffles normally empty into deep pools. Runs usually drain the downstream ends of pools, and these runs lead to successive riffles. This progression repeats itself as a stream winds through the countryside.

Rocks, logs, stumps, and weeds form attractive stream cover. Many stream fish like to hide under or close to cover and then dart out and grab a crawfish or minnow.

Analyzing a stream is a matter of studying the current, depth and cover. Remember that stream fish are consistent in the types of places where they hold. Catch one fish from behind a log, and chances are others will be hiding behind other logs.

Channel catfish and flatheads are found in deep pools in warm water streams. Catfish generally move deeper into pools as water temperatures rise toward midday.

Techniques for Fishing Small Streams

Information in the previous section addressed stream-fishing generalities. Now we get specific, learning exactly where to find different species and how to catch them.

In the process, understand that stream fish are more confined than lake or reservoir fish. In big waters, fish have a lot of room to move around, but in streams, they have to be somewhere along one narrow

waterway. Following are high-percentage methods for making fish bite.

BASS

Smallmouth bass are the predominant bass species found in many streams from the Mid-south into Canada. They hold in eddies behind or under cover adjacent to fast current. Typical spots would be behind a rock or a root wad that splits the current; beneath an undercut bank that lies beside a fast run; along edges (and especially ends) of weedbeds; or under a lip or rocky bar at the head of a pool where a riffle empties into it. I always pay special attention to holes gouged out where a stream makes a turn.

Smallmouth bass prefer shade to bright sunshine. Any place that offers quiet water and concealment with access to fast water is a potential smallmouth hot spot. Depth of such locations can vary. To fish these places, I recommend spinning or spin-cast tackle and 4- to 8-pound test line. You'll need something fairly light, because most stream smallmouth baits are small.

These fish feed mostly on craw-fish, minnows, worms, mature

insects and insect larvae. The best artificial baits imitate these natural foods. Small crawfish crankbaits are deadly. So are floating minnows, in-line spinners, small jigs (hair or rubber skirt) and 4-inch plastic worms (like the Slider). But my favorite lure for stream smallmouth is a brown tube lure rigged on a small jighead.

The key with all these baits is to work them close to cover. Cast your lure across or up the current, and work it right through the spot where you think bass might be holding. I like to swim a tube lure parallel to a log or deep-cut bank. I also like to crawl a crawfish crankbait or float a minnow lure over logs, rocks or stumps. I'll cast a jig into the head of a pool, allow it to sink, then hop it across bottom back through the heart of the pool. At times stream smallmouth will show a preference for one type bait. In early spring, floating minnows or in-line spinners seem to work best. Later on, tube lures, small crankbaits and jigs are better.

One of the secrets of catching stream smallmouth on artificial lures is accurate casting. You've got to get your lure close to the fish. When stream-fishing, wear camouflage or natural colors that won't spook fish. Ease in from a downstream or cross-stream position of where the fish should be. Use the current and your rod tip to steer the bait into the strike zone.

One note on float-fishing streams: when I see a place where smallmouth should be, I beach my canoe, get out and walk around the spot. Then I ease in close from the downstream side and start casting. It's easier to cast accurately while standing stationary instead of floating by a spot. Also, if I hook a fish, I can concentrate on playing it without worrying about controlling the canoe.

Smallmouth can be taken on several live baits, but crawfish and spring lizards are best. Use a slip-sinker rig (#1 hook) to work through high-percentage spots. Ease baits slowly along bottom, and set the hook at the first hint of a pickup.

Many slower, deeper streams will hold largemouth or spotted bass instead of smallmouth. Fish for largemouth and spotted bass just like you would for smallmouth. Cast around cover objects. Work the ends and edges of pools, and stay alert for any sign of feeding activity. If you see a bass chasing minnows, cast to that area immediately!

Tailwater areas beneath dams can be fishing hotspots. This is because fish migrating upstream can't get past the dam, so they congregate in the waters below it. Bass, white bass, stripers, catfish, sauger (shown here) and walleye are just a few of the many species that can be caught from tailwaters.

CATFISH

Channel and flathead catfish are common in warm-water streams. They usually stay in deep, quiet holes. When feeding, they move into current areas and watch for food washing by.

Fish pools, heads of pools or around cover in runs with moderate current. Use a bottom rig or a fixed-bobber rig and live bait. The weight of these rigs depends on the water depth and current.

Bait with worms, crawfish, fish guts, live minnows, cut bait or grasshoppers. Cast into the target zone, let the bait settle, and wait for a bite. Early and late in the day (or at night), concentrate on the heads of pools. During mid-day, work the deeper pools and mid-depth runs. Be patient.

WHITE BASS

White bass spend most of their lives in large lakes, reservoirs and rivers, but in spring, they make spawning migrations up tributary creeks.

This migration occurs as the water temperature approaches 60° F. Huge schools of white bass swim upstream to spawn in shallow riffles. Before and after spawning, these fish hold in eddy pools beside swifter water. They particularly like quiet pockets behind logjams or along the stream bank.

During this spawning run, white bass are very aggressive, and will hit almost any bait pulled by them. In-line spinners (white, chartreuse), leadhead jigs with plastic trailers, and small crankbaits are top choices. Retrieve them medium-fast, and keep moving until you locate fish. When you find them, slow down and work potential spots thoroughly.

TROUT

Trout are found in cold-water streams throughout much of the U. S. and Canada. Some are native to their home waters while others have been raised in hatcheries and stocked.

Fly-fishing is a popular, effective way to take trout, but I don't recommend it for beginners. I suggest sticking with light spinning tackle until you build your angling skills. Then you might "graduate" to fly-fishing in the future.

Stream trout are very elusive fish. Get too close, make too much noise, wear bright clothes, or drop a lure right on their heads, and they'll dart away. Instead, you have to stay back from feeding zones, remain quiet, wear drab-colored clothes, and cast beyond where you think the fish are.

Trout hold in similar areas as smallmouths. They prefer eddies adjacent to swift water where they can hide and then dart out to grab passing food. During insect hatches, trout also feed in open runs with moderate current.

Since most trout streams are clear, rig with 4- to 6-pound test line. Then tie on a small in-line spinner, spoon, floating minnow or crawfish crankbait. Cast these

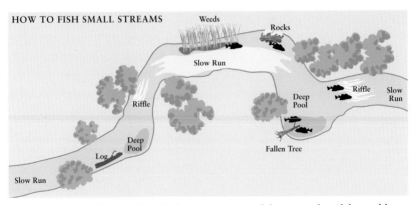

Streams, such as the one charted above, are some of the most plentiful – and least pressured – fishing spots in North America. This means that streamfish are naïve and easy to catch by anglers who know the basics of fishing these moving waters.

lures around rocks, logs, weeds and other likely structure bordering swift water. The heads of pools can be especially good early in the morning and late in the afternoon. Also, trout love to feed after dark.

Natural baits are also effective on stream trout. Night crawlers, salmon eggs, grasshoppers and minnows are good bets. Canned corn or small marshmallows will tempt bites, especially from hatchery-raised trout. All these baits should be fished on the bottom with a very small hook (#12) and a split shot clamped 10-12 inches up the line.

How to Fish Large Rivers

Earlier in this chapter I mentioned that fishing large lakes is like fishing small ponds in terms of basics. The same comparison can be made between small streams and large rivers. Big rivers are just little streams that have grown up. They are more complex, however, and contain a much broader range of fishing conditions.

Large rivers are the most diverse of all waters. They contain a wide variety of fishing locations: eddies, bluffs, dropoffs, shallow flats, feeder streams, backwater sloughs, tailwaters, deep and shallow areas,

and swift-flowing and calm water. Rivers also hold all species of freshwater fish and North American large rivers offer a smorgasbord of fishing opportunity.

As with small streams, large rivers are also divided into two types: warm and cold water. Most rivers in North America are the warm, deep variety, supporting sunfish, bass, white bass, catfish, walleye, etc. Many are dammed into "pools" to provide enough deep water for navigation.

In contrast, cold-water rivers are typically shallow and swift, flowing through mountainous areas and usually hold various trout species.

Large rivers are most often fished from boats, though you can fish successfully from the bank, especially below dams or in backwater sloughs and oxbows. But whichever method and location you choose, large rivers are topnotch fisheries that beginners and veteran anglers can share and enjoy.

Analyzing Large Rivers

As in small streams, current determines fish locations in large rivers. Understanding current and being able to read rivers is essential to fishing them.

Current in large rivers may be more difficult to figure out. In small streams you can see the riffles and swift runs, but in large rivers the current may appear equal from bank to bank. Look closer, though, and you'll see signs of current breaks. Points of islands, jetties, dam tailwaters, river bars and mouths of tributaries are all areas where current is altered, and are prime spots to catch fish.

Most fish in large rivers usually hang in eddies or slack water. Sometimes they prefer still water bordering strong current where they can ambush baitfish washing by. At other times they seek quiet backwater sloughs.

Besides current, three other variables in large rivers are water level, color, and cover.

WATER LEVEL – Rivers continuously rise and fall, depending on the amount of rainfall upstream. The level of the river is referred to as its "stage," and this can have

This stream angler is doing everything right. He's casting up-current, and retrieving his lure back through a deep hole with cover. There is a good chance he will get a strike from a bass or sunfish.

a direct bearing on fish locations. Many times, when a river is rising and its waters are flooding surrounding lowlands, fish move into these freshly-flooded areas to take advantage of a banquet of worms, crawfish and other food.

COLOR – Large rivers vary greatly in water clarity. While the main channel area may be muddy, backwaters can be clear and more attractive to fish. Or, entire river systems may be muddy or clear, depending on recent rains. Most fish species feed better in clear rather than muddy water.

COVER – Fish react to cover in rivers the same way they do in other bodies of water. Species such as bass, crappie and sunfish usually hold in or close to cover. Structure provides hiding places and a shield from current.

So when "reading" a large river, be aware of current (especially eddies), river stage, water color, and structure. You will encounter a broad range of combinations of these conditions that may confuse a beginning fisherman. But by following the advice in the remainder of this section, you can be assured that you're on track and that you can, indeed, mine large rivers of their fishing riches.

Techniques for Fishing Large Rivers

Many techniques for fishing large rivers are the same for ponds, lakes and small streams. Therefore, the key to catching fish from rivers is finding them and then applying the fundamentals of tackle, bait and fishing methods.

SUNFISH

Sunfish like quiet water, not current, so look for them in eddies, backwater sloughs, feeder creeks and other still areas. I've also caught sunfish from bridges, in quarries, gravel pits, riprap banks, tailwaters and other manmade spots. Remember that these fish won't linger in strong current very long, so find quiet, deep pools that have some structure.

Fish for them just like you would anywhere else. Use light tackle and small bobber rigs. Bait with worms, crickets or tiny tube jigs. Toss the bait right beside or into the cover, and wait for a bite.

When fishing for sunfish, many beginning anglers get frustrated because they get bites, but they can't hook the fish. There are two possible solutions: (1) try a smaller hook; (2) wait longer before setting the hook. If your bobber is dancing on the surface, wait for it to go completely under before setting the hook.

Crappie also prefer quiet water. The best places to find river crappie are sloughs and slow-moving tributaries. Sometimes crappie hold in treetops, brush and other cover along river banks where the current is slow to moderate in speed.

The best times to catch crappie in rivers are spring and fall, and the easiest way to catch them is to move from one piece of cover to the next. Use a long panfish pole and a fixed-bobber rig to drop a minnow or small crappie jig beside or into fallen treetops, brush or vegetation. Be quiet as you move, and get only as close to cover as you must to reach it with your pole. Work each new object thoroughly, covering all sides. Don't neglect areas where driftwood has collected. Sometimes river crappie hide under floating debris.

A special time for crappie is when a river is rising and flooding

Many cool-water streams in North America support abundant trout populations – both natives and stockers. The best way for beginners to catch these fish is casting tiny spinners or natural bait into holes below swift runs.

Basic Fishing Techniques 149

adjacent sloughs and creeks. As the river comes up, crappie move into cover in these areas. If your timing is good, you can work these freshly flooded areas for huge catches.

BASS

River bass receive far less angling pressure than lake and reservoir bass, which means there's some great fishing awaiting anglers who put forth the effort to find them.

In spring, look for river bass in quiet waters where current won't disturb their spawning beds. Cast to cover: brush, flooded timber, fallen trees, riprap banks, bridge pilings, etc. Spinnerbaits, buzz-baits, crankbaits, floating minnows and jigs are good lure choices.

By early summer, most river bass will move out to the main channel This is where the biggest concentrations of baitfish are found. Bass in current breaks can dart out and nail a hapless minnow passing by in the flow.

A broad variety of spots will hold river bass in summer and fall. These include: mouths of feeder creeks; eddies on the sides and downstream ends of islands; wash-ins and rock piles; ends and sides (upcurrent and downcurrent) of rock jetties (wing dams) that extend from the bank toward the channel; bridge pilings and riprap causeways; any tree or log washed up on a flat or bank; wing walls and breaks in riprap walls in tailwater areas. As in small streams, cast wherever the current is deflected by some object or feature in the river.

An increase in current can be a key to catching bass in a river. Many rivers have power dams and when the dams begin generating, the current increases suddenly. This rings the dinner bell for fish! Bass that have been inactive will move to ambush stations and start feeding with abandon.

Lure choices for fishing rivers run the gamut. Minnow-imitating crankbaits (diving and lipless) and buzz baits are good in eddy pools, sand and mud bars, rock piles and rock jetties. Spinnerbaits are a top choice for working logs, treetops, brush and weeds. Jigs tipped with a pork or plastic trailer will snare bass from tight spots close to cover. Select lures for rivers as you would in lakes.

When a river floods adjacent lowlands bass move into this fresh habitat to feed. Look for areas where the water is fairly clear and current is slack. Fish them with spinnerbaits, topwaters, shallow

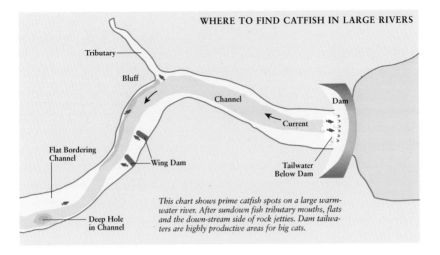

WHERE TO FIND CATFISH IN LARGE RIVERS

Tributary

Bluff

Channel

Dam

Current

Flat Bordering
Channel

Wing Dam

Tailwater
Below Dam

Deep Hole
in Channel

This chart shows prime catfish spots on a large warm-water river. After sundown fish tributary mouths, flats and the down-stream side of rock jetties. Dam tailwaters are highly productive areas for big cats.

crankbaits or plastic worms. When the water starts dropping, bass will abandon these areas and move back to deeper water. When the water starts dropping, cast around the downstream end of oxbows, sloughs and side channels.

Always be conscious of river bass "patterns." If you find fish at the mouth of a feeder creek, chances are the next creek will also hold bass. The same is true of jetties, islands, rocks, etc.

CATFISH/BULLHEADS

Catfish and bullheads are plentiful in most large warm-water rivers. In the daytime, catfish stay in deep holes and channel edges, while bullheads prefer shallower backwaters. At night, both roam actively in search of food.

The best time to try for these fish is just after sundown. Fish for catfish along bluffs, tributary mouths, flats bordering the channel, or the downstream side of rock jetties. Try for bullheads in mud-bottom sloughs.

For catfish, use stout tackle and a bottom rig. Sinkers should be heavy enough to keep the bait anchored in current (1-3 ounces). Hooks should be large and stout (1/0-3/0 steel). Live minnows, worms, cut bait, liver or any traditional catfish bait will work. Cast the rig and allow it to sink to the bottom. Prop the rod in a forked stick jammed and sit back and wait for a bite. Serious catfish anglers fish several rods at once. They stay in the same spot for several hours, waiting for the fish to feed.

A rock bank will offer red-hot catfishing during spawning time, especially if the rocks are out of direct current. Fish these spots with a fixed or slipbobber rig, adjusting the float so the bait hangs just above the rocks.

River catfishing can be phenomenal in dam tailwaters – a collection point for fish. Tailwaters contain baitfish, current, dissolved oxygen, and bottom structure where fish can hold and feed.

The best way to fish a tailwater is to work eddies close to the swift water that pours through the dam. If you're bank fishing, use a bottom rig and cast into quiet waters behind wing walls, pilings or the dam face. If the bottom is rough and you keep hanging up, switch to a slip-float rig adjusted so the bait hangs close to bottom.

A better way to fish tailwaters is from a boat, floating along current breaks while bumping a two-hook panfish rig off the bottom. Use enough weight so your line hangs almost straight under the boat. Make long downstream drifts, up to a quarter- mile or more, before

motoring back up to make another float. Don't lay your rod down since big catfish strike hard, and can yank it overboard.

Another special catfishing opportunity occurs right after a hard rain. Look for gulleys, drains or other spots where fresh water is rushing into the river. Catfish often move up below these inflows and feed furiously. In this case, use a fixed or slipbobber rig and dangle a bait only 2-3 feet under the surface in the immediate vicinity of the inflow.

Fish bullheads in rivers the same as in large lakes and reservoirs. Light tackle, worms and a bottom rig or bobber rig are hard to beat.

WALLEYE/SAUGER

Since these fish are similar, and the techniques to catch them are the same, I will mention only walleye, though the methods apply to both species.

River walleye collect in fairly predictable places. They spend most of their time out of current, so look for them around islands, rock jetties, eddies below dams, etc. They usually hold near the edge of an eddy where they can watch for food.

The best river conditions for catching walleye are when the water is low, stable and relatively clear. Walleye continue feeding when a river is rising, but may change locations in response to highwater conditions. When the river gets too muddy, or when the water starts dropping again, walleye generally become inactive and hard to catch.

Tailwaters below dams are the best places for beginners to catch river walleye. Some fish stay in tailwaters all year long, but the biggest concentrations occur during winter and early spring. Walleye may hold close to dam faces or behind wingwalls. They like to hang along rock ledges, gravel bars or other structure. But again, the key is reduced flow.

Boat-fishing is best for catching river walleye. Use a jig tipped with a live minnow, matching your jig weight to the amount of current. In slack water, a 1/8-ounce jig is heavy enough to work most tailwater areas. Float or troll through likely walleye locations, vertically jigging off the bottom. Or anchor and cast into eddies, holes and current breaks. Let the jig sink to the bottom, and work it back with a lift/drop retrieve. At all times, work the bait slowly. Set the hook at the slightest bump.

A good technique for bank fishermen is casting crankbaits or jigs tipped with minnows along riprap banks in early spring. Walleye spawn along the rocks downstream from dams when the water temperature climbs into the mid-40° F range. Cast parallel to banks, bump crankbaits off the rocks, or swim jigs just above them.

In summer and fall, look for walleye farther downstream, along riprap banks, jetties, gravel or rock bars, mouths of tributaries or sloughs, or deep eddy pools at the edge of current. Cast jigs or troll live-bait rigs through deeper areas, or cast crankbaits along rocky shallows.

WHITE BASS/STRIPERS/ HYBRIDS

These three species of fish share similar river habitats and patterns. Since white bass are the most common, I will refer only to them. But be aware that where stripers and hybrids coexist with white bass, you may catch any of the three.

In the section on how to fish small streams, I mentioned the white bass spawning run. These fish also spawn in tailwaters below dams on large rivers, and at this time fishing is easy and productive.

White bass move into tailwaters and feed actively in early spring, when the water temperature rises into the low 50° F. range.

One good way to catch them is to cast jigs from the bank. Use ⅛-ounce jigs in light current and ¼-ounce jigs in strong current. Dress the jigs with plastic curly-tail trailers (white, yellow, chartreuse). Experiment by casting into both eddies and current, by allowing your jig to sink to different levels before starting the retrieve; and by varying your retrieve speed. Once you find a good pattern, stick with it. When you find tailwater white bass in early spring, you can catch them by the dozen!

After they spawn, white bass move back downstream. In summer and fall, they feed in large open areas of a river. If dams along the river generate electricity, white bass feeding activity will be affected by the generation schedule. When the generators go on and the current increases, feeding begins. Some dams publish daily generation schedules, and smart anglers check them to time their trips to coincide with when the current is running.

White bass feed where current washes baitfish into shallow or confined areas. Flats on outside bends of a river, upstream points of islands, ends of jetties, sand or gravel bars, or ledges adjacent to tributary mouths are all good locations.

Cast to these areas with jigs, spoons, in-line spinners, chrome-finish lipless crankbaits, or any lure that simulates a small baitfish. Always be alert for surface feeding. Cast into the middle of any surface activity and reel in quickly. Sometimes white bass will come up and froth the surface while chasing minnows.

NORTHERN PIKE

Use the same tactics, tackle and baits for pike in large rivers that you would use in large lakes and reservoirs. The only difference is locating these fish within the river system.

The best places to look for river pike are in backwaters. They often hold in sloughs, marshes, tributaries and oxbows away from the main channel. Cast to logs, brush or other shallow cover.

As in lakes and reservoirs, river pike are most active in spring, early summer and fall. A bonus time to fish for pike is whenever a river is rising and flooding adjacent lowlands. If you stay on the move and make a lot of casts, you're likely to enjoy some first-rate pike action.

A catfisherman fishes two rods at sunset. Catfish are active nighttime feeders and will leave deeper water to roam bluffs, flats and creek mouths in search of food.

TROUT

Many large cold-water rivers offer very good trout fishing. Deep runs can harbor lunker browns, rainbows and cutthroats. These trophy fish are very wary, so they're hard for beginning anglers to catch. However, smaller trout can provide plenty action for beginners who use basic techniques and who are careful not to spook the fish.

As in small streams, current is the most important factor in deciding where to try for trout in large rivers. The concept is simple. Current funnels food into predictable areas, and the fish hold in or around these areas where the pickings are easy. They'll lie in the shadows and then dart out and grab a morsel as it drifts by.

Pools below riffles or waterfalls are prime feeding locations. So are eddies behind rocks, logs or anything else that diverts current. Undercut, shaded banks on outside bends of the river are prime hiding places for trout as are holes below the mouths of feeder creeks. The trick is to study the current for places next to the flow where trout can lurk and watch for food.

Fish these spots with the same lures recommended for stream trout: spinners, spoons, floating minnows and small crankbaits. Always cast upstream and retrieve your lure back with the current. Decide exactly where you think trout should be and pull your lure close to this location.

Use natural bait the same way as in small streams. Worms, minnows, grasshoppers and salmon eggs will take native trout. Whole kernel corn, cheese, and small marshmallows are good for stocked trout. Fish these baits with a small hook and a split shot crimped a foot above the hook. Make a quartering cast upstream from where the trout should be. Then reel in slack line and feel for a bite as the current carries the bait along bottom. Set the hook at any unnatural bump or pressure.

Summary

In this chapter we've covered a lot of ground, or should we say water? If you've read this entire chapter without trying any of these techniques, you're probably shaking your head and saying, "No way! It's too much." That intimidation factor is setting in again.

But you won't digest fishing by taking big bites. Instead, take little bites, and chew thoroughly. Pick one small part of fishing, one location and species, and learn this before moving on. Then take another bite, and another, and so on until you're an accomplished angler who can match techniques to changing locations and conditions.

Fishing success breeds confidence, and confidence breeds success. Start simple to build confidence. Then gradually move to other species and more advanced techniques.

One of the great pleasures for a beginner is catching fish because he knew what to do and did it properly instead of being "lucky." If you follow the instructions in this chapter and practice them, you'll catch fish, and you'll gain the confidence and sense of accomplishment that veteran anglers enjoy.

Now, let's move forward to Chapter 9 and learn what to do once you get 'em to bite.

How to Play, Land, and Handle Fish

In all my years of bass fishing, I've never caught a 10-pounder, but I think I had one hooked a few years ago on a reservoir near my home. The month was March, and the weather was unseasonably warm. Largemouth responded to the sudden rise in water temperature by going on a feeding spree. It was pre-spawn, and the big females were in along the banks gorging on crawfish before moving onto their beds.

"Playing" and "fighting" fish mean the same thing: using the rod to tire them out so you can land them. Beginning anglers must learn to exert just enough pressure with their tackle to wear a hooked fish down without risking breaking their line.

I was casting shallow rocky areas with a crankbait. I'd caught several fish, including a couple of 5-pounders. Then on one cast, my lure simply stopped, like it had lodged between two rocks. I held pressure on my line just to be sure, and suddenly I felt movement. I set back with my rod, and that's when the fight of my fishing life started. This bass was too big to jump. Instead, she boiled on the surface and pulled like a freight train. I couldn't gain any line. I just held on and prayed that my drag would work until this fish tired, then I'd reel her to the side of the boat.

This battle lasted a couple of minutes; it seemed like an hour! I finally had her coming my way. I was playing her very carefully, not exerting too much pressure to break my line or pull the hooks out. Once, when she cruised by the boat, I got a good look at her, and she was a giant! Truly, she was 10 pounds if an ounce. Then she made one more headshake, and the lure popped free! I watched her slowly swim away, and my heart sank as she disappeared down into the water. I'll never forget the excitement of that fight or the dejection I felt when she got away.

Truly, one of the great thrills in fishing is hooking and playing a big fish, and one of the heartbreaks is losing it! All fishermen want to catch a big one. It's an integral part of the sport. And all fishermen taste disappointment when a lunker comes off, even when they would have released it alive if they'd landed it. Still, it's the uncertainty of this sport that makes it exciting. If you knew you'd land every fish

you hooked, fishing wouldn't be nearly as much fun.

This isn't to say that you shouldn't try to land every fish you hook. You should, and this is why you need to learn proper playing, landing and handling methods. By using the right techniques, you'll enjoy the "thrill of victory" more often. This chapter will explain these techniques. In the following pages, you'll learn to play a fish to keep the odds in your favor; how to land fish from a boat or on shore; and how to handle fish both for your safety and their well being in case you want to turn them back alive.

Fine Art of "Playing Fish"

"Playing" fish and "fighting" fish mean the same thing. These are terms for tiring a fish out and reeling it close enough to capture. Playing small fish is easy; they don't have as much size or fight. However, playing a big fish can be a tough head-tohead battle. If you don't know what you're doing, you'll lose more of these contests than you'll win.

There are two overall "concepts" for playing fish. One is to play them with the main purpose of having fun, of stretching the fight

Using a landing net is a safe, effective way to land fish once they have been played down. The proper technique is to hold the net just beneath the water's surface, guide the fish over the net headfirst, then lift with the net to trap the fish inside. Never stab or swipe with a net at a fish that's swimming by the boat.

out and giving the fish maximum opportunity to get away. Anglers who like to do this frequently use light or ultra light tackle because it takes more finesse to land fish with light tackle. Due to the lack of strength in this tackle, you don't have as much control over the fish. You can't power them in, so you have to wear them down more. The longer a fight lasts, the greater the odds of the fish getting away.

Using light tackle gives a fish more of a sporting chance. Many anglers use light tackle because they like the challenge of playing and landing big fish with whippy rods and thin line.

The second way to play fish is with the purpose of landing them as fast and efficiently as possible. These anglers have a saying: "You can play with them after you get them in the boat." They are more

Each angler must decide which approach he prefers. Neither is more or less acceptable than the other. They are just different playing styles for different purposes and philosophies.

concerned with the end result – landing fish – than how they land them. Tournament anglers or those fishing for food are more likely to use these "power" methods, which typically involve heavier tackle and stronger line.

Pointers for Playing Fish

Following are pointers for playing large bass, walleye, stripers, pike, catfish, muskies and other big fish.

Rule number one is to keep the line tight at all times. This is no

Handling Fish

When handling fish you've just caught, always be alert to possible injury from fins, teeth, spines, or exposed hooks. Maintain a firm grip on the fish as you remove the hooks. I always keep needle nose pliers handy to remove hooks. You can get a better hold and apply more force to hooks embedded in bony tissue. Also, using pliers keeps your hand away from exposed hooks if the fish flops.

If fish are to be released alive, they must be handled carefully so they can be returned to the water in good shape. (A thorough look at catch-and-release, when it's okay to keep fish, and when they should be released alive – follows in the next chapter.)

If you intend to release a fish alive, special care must start when you're playing it. Land the fish as soon as possible, without completely tiring it out. Total exhaustion cuts down on its chances for survival.

After landing the fish, handle it as little as possible, and put it back in the water quickly. Handling removes protective slime from the fish's body, which increases chances for bacterial growth and eventual death. Keeping a fish out of the water too long also causes oxygen shortage, which can put the fish into shock. It's okay to admire it briefly or snap a photo, but then place it gently back in the water in a swimming position and let it go. (Don't flop the fish back into the water carelessly.) If the fish rolls belly up instead of swimming off, retrieve the fish and hold it right sideup in the water to see if it will revive. If it swims off under its own power, it'll probably survive. If it doesn't swim away after a minute or two, keep the fish to eat. It's probably been injured in the fight and will die, so keep and use the fish rather than waste it.

problem if the fish is pulling against you. But if it's running toward you, reel in line fast enough to keep out slack. When a fish jumps, it's easier for it to throw a lure or hook if the line is slack. Therefore, when a fish goes airborne, keep the line tight to control headshakes. Also, many expert anglers try to prevent or control jumps by keeping the rod tip low or even poking it down in the water when a fish starts up. Sometimes this downward pressure will cause the fish to turn back down.

When fighting a fish, use the bend of the rod to tire it out. Except during jumps (when you're pointing the rod down), hold the rod or pole high with maximum bend. Many pros hold their rod with both hands tight to their chest, which is a very strong fighting position. Sometimes you can also hold a rod sideways or over your head for more leverage.

You must adjust your playing technique to the type tackle you're using. Obviously, if you're using light tackle, you can't exert as much pressure on fish as you can with heavier tackle. On the other hand, if you're fishing around thick cover (brush, weeds, standing timber, boat docks, etc.), you may have to apply maximum pressure on a fish

to keep it from burrowing in and tangling your line. You should consider using heavier tackle and line when fishing around thick cover. This will allow you to apply more pressure to turn a fish away from the cover.

With really big fish, a pump-and-reel technique works well. Lift slowly and steadily with the rod to raise the fish. Then reel in line

Many anglers prefer the challenge of fighting a fish using light tackle combined with thin line and a very flexible rod.

as you lower your rod back down. Do this over and over – lifting, then taking slack. Repeating this process keeps constant pressure on a fish and tires it quickly. When pumping and reeling, always keep the line tight. In this situation, slack in the line usually translates into a fish that gets away.

Probably the biggest mistake anglers make in playing fish is getting in too big a hurry. They try to reel it in too fast. If you "overplay" a fish, you risk pulling the hook out or breaking your line. Instead, unless a fish is headed into thick cover, keep steady pressure and be patient. Let the fish tire out before you attempt to land it. Simply hold onto the fish while it's fighting, and then start reeling as it plays out.

How to Set and Use Drag

"Drag" is an elemental concept in playing fish, and it's one that all rod-and-reel anglers must learn to use. Basically, drag is a slip-clutch mechanism built into a reel that allows line to slip out when a pre-set amount of pressure is exerted on the line. It is a safeguard against pulling so hard against a fighting fish that you break your line. Drag settings are adjustable, and drag should be set at some point below the break strength of the line you're using. Then, when a fish applies this amount of pull, the drag will slip and give line rather than allowing pressure to build to the breaking point.

Let's apply this to a practical fishing situation. Say you're using 8-pound test line. You might set your drag to slip when 6 pounds of pressure is applied to the line. Then, if you hook a big fish and it makes a strong run, the drag will give before the line snaps. Then, as the fish tires and stops pulling drag, you can reel in line and land the fish.

When a fish is pulling out drag, don't continue turning the reel handle, since this causes line twist in the reel. Instead, hold the reel handle steady until the fish stops running or until it turns back toward you. Then begin reeling again to keep tension on the line as you play the fish.

Two Methods for Setting Drag

Setting the proper amount of drag can be a complicated process. Several factors go into knowing how much drag is just right. Strength of the line, weight and strength of the fish, how much line

Ethics on the Water
Obey all boating laws.
These laws are designed
to protect you and other
boaters. Observe "no
wake" zones and practice
common courtesy by not
running your boat too
close to a stationary boat
or to anglers fishing from
the bank.

*Bass don't have teeth, so they can be held and
lifted by the lower jaw. Insert your thumb in a
bass' mouth, clamp the lower jaw between your
thumb and forefinger, and lift the fish from the
water.*

is out, and the amount of line on the reel spool all affect how much drag is needed. Also, conditions that determine the optimum drag setting can change rapidly when fighting a fish.

Obviously, you won't know these variables before you start fishing, so drag must be pre-set according to the "best guess" method. Many fishing experts set drag to give at half the rated break strength of the line. For instance, for 6-pound test line, set the drag to slip at 3 pounds of pressure. This may be slightly on the light side, but it provides a good margin for error.

The first method for setting drag is more precise than the second,

How to Play, Land, and Handle Fish 163

but it takes more effort. Tie one end of a small fish-weighing scale to an unmovable object like a tree or post. Then tie your fishing line to the other end. Disengage the reel spool or trip the bail and back away approximately 20 yards. Then re-engage the spool or bail. Hold the rod at a 90-degree angle to the scale (just like you're fighting a fish), and reel the line tight. Then start pulling the line with the rod while adjusting the drag setting. Have a friend watch the scale and tell you when you're pulling out the desired amount of pressure. Adjust the drag so it slips at this weight. Then it's properly set.

The other method for setting drag, the one used by most fishermen, is the "feels-right" method. You simply run the line through the rod guides. Then hold the rod handle with one hand and pull the line off the reel with the other. Adjust the drag setting to slip before the line snaps. This feels-right method of setting drag isn't nearly as accurate as using the scale, but it's much faster.

Also, remember that you can readjust drag setting whenever you wish while actually fighting a fish. Baitcasting and spin-cast reels have star drags next to the reel handle that can be tightened or loosened as desired. Spinning reels have knobs either on the front of the spool or behind the gearbox that can be turned to tighten or loosen drag as desired.

Drags have a tendency to stick when reels haven't been used for a long time. When storing your reel, adjust the drag to a very loose setting. Then reset and test drag before each new fishing trip. When working properly, drag will yield line smoothly instead of in spurts. Overall, knowing how to use drag properly is a mark of an accomplished fisherman. Proper use of drag will allow you to catch many more fish in the course of your angling career.

How to Land Fish

Landing a fish is the end result of playing it. This is the actual capture, when you net, grab or beach a fish. If you know what you're doing, landing is easy. Regardless of where or how you're fishing, the number one rule in landing is to make sure the fish is tired out. Too many anglers try to land fish while they are "green" (they still have some fight left), and the fish escapes in a last-ditch lunge. So play a fish down to the point where it's easier to handle. (An exception

Caring for Fish for Taxidermy Purposes

Many anglers enjoy reliving their fishing memories through taxidermy mounts. Possibly the best option for this is to have your taxidermist do a replica mount. When you boat a trophy fish, quickly measure its length (nose to tail) and girth (around the body behind the gills and behind the dorsal fin. Next take a close-up photo of the fish and release it alive. A good taxidermist can take your measurements and photo and make an exact replica of your trophy, and the fish will live to spawn – and perhaps thrill some other angler – another day.

Still, if you prefer to have the actual fish mounted, here's how to handle it. First, take a close-up photo to serve as a reference for painting. Next, wrap the fish in a wet towel or newspapers and place it in a shady, out-of-the-way spot. Don't put the fish on a stringer or in a cooler where scales might be knocked off.

When you get home, lay the fish on a small plywood board. Wrap it in several layers of plastic wrap, and seal it in a plastic garbage bag. Then deposit the fish in the freezer until it can be transported to the taxidermist. The board will protect the tail and fins from accidental breakage, and the plastic wrapping will prevent freezer burn. With careful handling, your mount is more likely to return looking alive and natural, providing many pleasant memories in the years to come.

to this rule is when you intend to release the fish alive.)

If you're fishing from the bank, and the bank slopes gently into the water, simply drag the fish onto land. If the bank is steep, or if you're fishing from a boat, lift the fish out of the water with your rod or pole. To do this, however, you must be using line that has a higher pound-test rating than the weight of the fish. If you try to lift a 6-pound bass with 4-pound line, the line will break.

When beaching or lifting a fish, it helps to have the fish's momentum going in the direction you're trying to move it. If the fish is swimming, you can steer it up on the bank or into shallow water where you can grab it. I once used this method to beach a 25-pound pike that I'd hooked on light spinning tackle and 8-pound test line.

Nets are great for landing fish from the bank, from a boat or when wading. The netting procedure is always the same. After the fish is played down and under control, lift its head out of the water with gentle rod pressure. Then lead the fish headfirst into a stationary net held just below the water's surface. When the fish is in or over the net, lift up. Never chase or stab at a fish with a landing net, and never attempt to net a fish tail-first. Both mistakes will cause you to lose many fish.

A third common way to land fish is by hand. In doing so, you must be extremely careful. Sharp fins, teeth, spines and gill plates can inflict painful injuries. Also, if a fish isn't played down, an illtimed headshake can embed loose hooks in your hand.

There are two ways to land fish by hand. Species that don't have teeth (bass, stripers, crappie, etc.) can be grabbed and lifted by the lower jaw. To do this, reel the fish up close and lift its head out of the water with rod pressure. Then stick your thumb in the fish's mouth, clamp the lower jaw between your thumb and forefinger, and lift the fish from the water.

Species that do have teeth (pike, walleye, muskie) should be grabbed across the back, pinching firmly on both gill plates. They may also be lifted by placing a hand under the belly. In either case, the fish must be played down fully before you attempt to land it.

Anglers handling catfish should be careful of these fish's sharp dorsal spine. A moment of carelessness can lead to a painful puncture wound in the hand.

Many anglers also land fish by inserting their fingers into the gills or by squeezing thumb and forefinger into the fish's eye sockets. These methods work, but they are not recommended. Some species have very sharp gill plates that can inflict a nasty cut if the fish flops. Also, if a fish is to be released alive, its gills or eyes can be damaged by such rough treatment.

CHAPTER 10

Simple Methods for Cleaning and Cooking Fish

One of the real pleasures in life is "shore lunch" – beaching your boat and cooking and eating fish that you've just caught. Fresh fillets cooked over an open fire are always delicious. A morning of fishing guarantees a hearty appetite, and the fish will never be fresher or taste better. Throw in a skillet of home-fried potatoes and onions, baked beans warmed in the can, some shredded cabbage and cole slaw dressing, and some deep-fried hushpuppies, and you have a meal that rivals those served in the finest restaurants. Ah, the memories of shore lunches past!

Fish fillets never taste better than when cleaned, cooked and served up as shore lunch right beside the water where they were caught.

For many anglers, eating fish is the end process and final reward in fishing. Fish are delicious, and they're more healthful than red meat, particularly when baked or broiled. There's a special satisfaction in sharing your catch with fishing buddies or other friends.

However, for fish to taste their best, they must be cleaned and cooked properly. This process starts the moment the fish is landed. First, however, let's discuss when to keep fish and when to release them.

To Keep or Release?

Catch-and-release is fishing for fun instead of for food. Releasing fish alive protects the resource against too much fishing pressure. Fish that are turned back alive can continue spawning, maintaining healthy populations, and providing fun and excitement for other anglers. Some anglers feel morally bound to release their catch alive, and they encourage others to do likewise.

So, is it okay to keep some fish to eat, and if so, when? Let's get one point straight. Fish are renewable resources. If managed properly, a certain number of fish can be taken from a population, and remaining fish can continue replenishing the population from one spawning season to the next. If certain criteria are met, anglers should feel no stigma in keeping fish to eat.

So, when is it okay to keep fish to eat, and when should you release them alive? There are two sides to this question: legal and moral. Legally, you may keep your catch (1) if you have a fishing license; (2) take your fish by lawful methods; and (3) comply with creel and length limits.

Morally, the question of catch-and-release is a little more complicated. Some purists feel you should release every fish you catch. On the other end of the spectrum are fish hogs who keep every fish they get.

Simply stated, you should decide to keep or release your fish according to how plentiful they are and how heavy fishing pressure is. If fish are plentiful and pressure is light, it's okay to keep your catch. On the other hand, if fish are scarce or under extreme fishing pressure, anglers should release their catch – with one exception: a fish that's injured and will probably die It's good conservation to keep these fish.

Remember back to Chapter 3 and my secret smallmouth stream? Let's use it as an example of how to decide whether or not to keep fish or release them.

This stream holds a healthy bass population, and I've never seen another angler on it. I fish it only twice a year, so I have no

The fresher fish are, the better they'll taste when cooked. One good way to keep fish fresh is to string them (when water temperature is cool.) Another good way is to kill fish quickly and deposit them on ice in a cooler.

qualms about keeping enough fish for a couple of meals. The removal a small number of bass has no effect on the overall number of smallmouth in this stream.

But let's say the stream was suddenly discovered by other anglers, and fishing pressure became heavy. If I saw evidence of fishing pressure hurting the smallmouth population, I'd start releasing all my fish alive, and would encourage other anglers to do likewise.

As a general guideline, prolific breeders such as sunfish, crappie, perch, bullheads, catfish and white bass are less likely to be hurt by fishing pressure, so it's usually okay to keep these species. It's the bass, walleye, trout, muskies and other trophy fish that suffer most from fishing pressure. Depending on population and pressure in each situation, these are the species that should be considered for live release, especially the big female fish. These spawners are important in maintaining high population numbers.

If you do choose to keep fish to eat, keep the smaller fish; keep only what you need; and release the rest. Even when fish are plentiful, don't be wasteful.

Caring for Your Catch

When you keep fish to eat, be sure they stay fresh. This guarantees they will retain their best flavor for cooking. If fish aren't kept fresh, the flesh becomes mushy and strong-tasting.

There are two ways to ensure freshness: keep fish alive; or keep them cold. Fish may be kept alive in a fish basket, on a stringer or in the live well of a boat if the water is cool and well-oxygenated. Or, fish may be killed and placed on ice as soon as they're caught.

When you fish from the bank, a simple rope or chain stringer is the easiest way to keep your catch. Punch the point of the stringer up through the fish's mouth; then pull the stringer through the open mouth. Do not string fish through the gills. This makes it hard for them to breathe and could cause them to die. In hot weather, it's better to put fish on ice rather than trying to keep them alive on a stringer.

Ethics & Etiquette

Manners Afloat If you're in a boat fishing along a bank, and you come upon someone fishing from shore, make a wide circle around his spot without fishing it. He only has that one small area, you have the rest of the lake.

Dead fish that aren't placed on ice will spoil quickly. Check the eyes and gill color to determine freshness. If the eyes look clear and the gills are dark red, the fish are fresh. If the eyes are cloudy and the gills have turned pinkish-white, the fish are beginning to spoil.

Before putting fish in a cooler, give them a sharp rap with a blunt object (pliers, knife handle, etc.) on the spine just behind the eyes. This kills them quickly, which keeps them from flopping when placed in the cooler. Then place the fish on top of a bed of crushed ice in the cooler. Keep excess water drained away as the ice melts. Fish flesh gets mushy when soaked in water for an extended time.

Many anglers prefer to field-dress their fish before placing them on ice. This is done by cutting the gills and guts away with a small knife. These are the organs that spoil first, so this additional step helps ensure freshness.

Simple Methods for Cleaning Fish

Fish should be cleaned as soon after they're caught as possible. Don't leave fish in a cooler overnight. Clean and refrigerate them immediately. They will taste better, and you'll be glad you don't have to face this cleaning chore the next day.

There are a number of options for cleaning fish. They can be scaled or skinned with the bones left intact, or they can be filleted (meat cut away from the bones). It's up to each angler's preference. Usually small fish (bluegill, perch) are scaled and cooked whole, but even they can be filleted. When fish are filleted by a skilled cleaner, little useable meat is wasted.

Tools for Cleaning Fish

Any fish-cleaning method requires a sharp knife. I recommend one of the fillet knives sold in sporting goods stores. These knives have thin, sharp, flexible blades for fast,

Filleting is a simple, easy way to prepare larger fish for cooking. Anglers using this cleaning method can quickly remove bones and skin from the meat. The first step is to slice the fillet lengthwise down the backbone, from the gills to the tail.

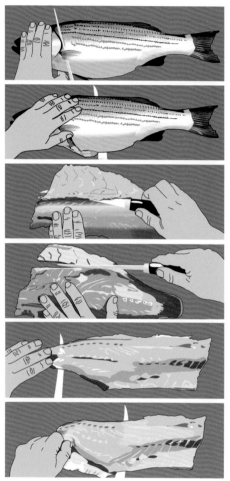

To fillet (1) Cut behind the pectoral fin to the backbone. (2) Separate the fillet, cutting toward the tail parallel to the backbone. (3) Cut off the rib section by sliding the blade along the bones. (4) Cut off the belly fat. (5) With the skin side down, begin to cut from the tail (6) Cut the skin from the fillet with a sawing motion ...

easy cleaning. A knife with a 7-inch blade is adequate for cleaning most pan- and gamefish.

One good option to a fillet knife is an electric knife. Run by batteries or power cord, an electric knife is a great fish-cleaning tool. Anyone can learn to use an electric knife to fillet fish with just a little practice. Of course, fish cleaners must be careful not to cut themselves, and this is an even greater concern with an electric knife.

An inexpensive metal scaler with pointed teeth makes scaling fish much easier, but scaling can also be done with a metal spoon or a kitchen knife with a rigid blade. A fish-cleaning glove is optional; it protects your hand from nicks. A piece of 1/2-inch plywood makes a good cleaning platform, and you'll need two pans or buckets: one for the cleaned fish, and the other for discarded remains.

Fishermen also need "tools" for removing the fish smell from their hands. Commercial soaps are sold for this purpose. Also, rubbing your hands in toothpaste will remove fish smell. Then, a coating of lemon juice will add a refreshing scent. (Beware rubbing your hands in lemon juice if you have nicks or cuts!)

Scaling

Scaling is the process of scraping the scales off fish and then removing the heads and guts. The skin is left on, and all bones remain intact. Smaller sunfish, crappie, perch, walleye, bass, white bass and other species can all be scaled and cooked whole.

To scale a fish, lay it on its side. Hold its head with one hand, and scrape from the tail to the head (against the grain). The sides are easy to scale. The difficult spots are along the back and stomach and close to the fins.

After scaling, cut the head off just behind the gills. Then slice the belly open and remove the guts. The tail and major fins may be cut off if desired. Finally, wash the fish thoroughly to remove loose scales and blood.

Filleting

Many anglers prefer to fillet their fish for meat with no bones. Fish cleaned in this manner are easy to cook and a pleasure to eat. Also, when filleting is mastered, it's faster than scaling. Experts can fillet a fish in less than a minute. The only drawback is losing a small amount of meat in the filleting process.

Skinning is the preferred way for cleaning catfish and bullheads. After a large catfish is skinned, it may be cut into steaks for ease in cooking.

To fillet a fish, place it on its side and hold the head with one hand. Make a cut behind the pectoral fin (the fin behind the gill plate). This cut should be from top to bottom of the fish and as deep as the backbone. Then roll the knife blade toward the tail, and begin cutting parallel to the backbone with a sawing motion. (Keep the knife close to the backbone.) Done properly, this will cut through the ribs and separate the entire side of meat from the fish. Stop cutting just in front of the tail, leaving the meat attached to the body.

Next, lay the fillet back over the tail with the skin side lying flat against the cleaning board. Cut through the meat at the base of the fillet, but don't cut through the skin. Instead, roll the knife edge flat to the skin, and begin cutting between the skin and meat, separating the skin from the fillet. With a pulling-sawing motion, work the length of the fillet to separate the skin from the meat.

Now you have a side of meat with the skin removed, but the rib bones are still in the fillet. The last step is to cut around the rib section with the point of the knife to remove it from the fillet.

Each side of the fish is filleted in this manner. The end result will be two boneless slabs of meat, which should be washed and refrigerated immediately.

Skinning

Catfish and bullheads are covered by a slick skin instead of scales. These fish may be filleted as explained above, but many anglers prefer to skin and gut them. Catfish and bullheads may then be cooked whole, or bigger fish may be cut into steaks.

To skin a catfish, lay it on its stomach. Grip the head firmly with one hand, carefully avoiding the side and top spines, which can inflict painful puncture wounds. Slit the skin along both sides just behind the pectoral spines. Then slice the skin from the back of the head along both sides of the dorsal (top) fin to the point where the fin ends. Then, with a firm grip on the head, use pliers to grasp the skin at the point where these two cuts meet, and peel the skin back down the body and over the tail. Skin both sides in this manner. Then cut the head off, remove the guts, wash and refrigerate.

Simple Tips for Cooking Fish

Cooking and eating fish is the end result of the harvesting process. It gives me great pleasure to catch fish, cook them and serve them to close friends. Following are simple tips for preparing fish.

FRYING – Frying is probably the most popular way to cook fish. Fish can be fried whole or in steaks or fillets. I prefer to fry fillets, and I cut fillets into chunks no larger than a couple of inches square.

Bread the fish before frying. Fish may be breaded with crushed saltines or corn flakes, bread crumbs, biscuit mix or commercial fish breadings. Far and away

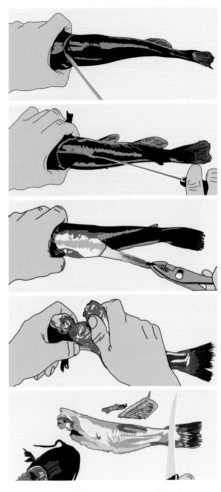

Skinning catfish. (1) Grip the head and slit the skin on both sides just behind the pectoral spines. (2) Slice the skin along the backbone to just behind the dorsal fin. (3) Use pliers to peel the skin off over the tail. (4) Pull the head down breaking the backbone and pull out the guts. (5) Remove the fins with pliers and slice off the tail.

Storing Fish for Cooking

Fish can be kept in the refrigerator for 2-3 days without losing much freshness. However, if longer storage is desired, they should be frozen.

To keep cleaned fish (whole, fillets or steaks) in the refrigerator, blot them dry with a paper towel. Then place them on a plate covered with paper towels and wrap them tightly with plastic wrap.

To freeze whole fish, place them inside a plastic milk jug (cut the top away) or large frozen food container, then cover them with water. Tap the sides of the container to release trapped air. Use masking tape to label the container with the type fish and date they were caught. Then freeze.

To freeze fillets or steaks, place fish pieces in a double-walled Ziploc freezer bag (one bag inside another). Zip the inner bag almost closed, and suck all air out of this bag to form a vacuum seal around the fish. Then zip the inner bag closed. Do the same with the outer bag. The double thickness protects against freezer burn. Before freezing, label the outer bag with the type fish and date they were caught.

Fish frozen in either manner described above will keep 6 months or longer without losing their fresh flavor.

To thaw whole fish frozen in ice, run tap water over the container until the block of ice can be removed. Place this frozen block in a colander or a dish drainer so melting water can drain. Thaw fish at room temperature. To thaw bagged fillets, place in a baking pan and thaw at room temperature. Cook fish as soon as possible after they're thawed.

the most popular breading is yellow corn meal or a corn meal/flour mix. Either of these breadings fries to a thin, golden brown crust that doesn't overpower the taste of the fish.

I use peanut oil for frying fish, and I deep-fry them in a cast iron Dutch oven on a fish cooker. The secret to delicious, crispy fish is having the oil hot enough before you drop the fish in, and then keeping it hot as you cook. The ideal temperature for frying fish is 375° F.

Fillets are thin, they won't take long to cook. Whole fish will take longer. When deep-frying, individual pieces are done when they float to the top of the bubbling oil. When pan-frying, cook the fish until they are golden brown; flip them over and cook them the same amount of time on the other side. Test for flakiness with a fork. When they are done, place them on a platter covered with paper towels to absorb oil, and serve them immediately.

BAKING – Baking is a healthy alternative to frying, and it is an almost foolproof method for cooking fish. Lightly grease the bottom of a baking dish. Arrange whole fish, fillets or steaks in the dish. Brush them with a mixture of melted butter and lemon juice. For variety, add garlic powder, Italian dressing, soy sauce or cajun seasoning. Put the lid on the fish or seal it with aluminum foil, and place the dish in an oven preheated to 375° F.

A standard-size baking dish of fish will bake in 15-25 minutes, depending on the size and thickness of the pieces. Baste the fish with the lemon-butter mixture once or twice while baking. Test for doneness by inserting a fork into the thickest part of the fish to check for flakiness. Do not over-bake fish; they will dry out. When the fish are ready to serve,

baste them once more with the hot lemon-butter.

CHAR-GRILLING – More and more anglers are discovering the ease and good taste of charcoalgrilled fish. This simple cooking method takes little time and effort. It does require a grill with a hood or top to hold in smoke and regulate temperature. I prefer large fillets for grilling. but whole fish can also be char-grilled.

Light the charcoal and wait for the briquettes to burn down to an ash-gray color. Then add water-soaked hickory or mesquite chips for a smoky flavor.

When the fire is ready, spread heavy-duty aluminum foil over just enough of the grill to hold the fish. Then place the fillets skin-side down on the foil. Baste them with lemon-butter, barbeque sauce, Italian dressing or any other moist

seasoning. Lower the top over the grill and regulate the air control so the charcoal will smolder and smoke at a low temperature. Baste the fish at intervals while cooking. Do not turn fillets; leave them with the skin down. Test for doneness by inserting a fork into the thickest part of the fish, and twist to see if the meat is flaky. Cooking time will vary depending on the size of fish and heat of the fire. Chargrilling fillets usually takes only a few minutes.

To char-grill whole fish, do not use foil. Place the fish directly on the grill or in a wire grilling basket. Turn the fish to cook an equal time on each side.

Many anglers prefer filleting over other cleaning methods. Filleting produces boneless, skinless pieces of fish that are ready to be cooked.

Summary

There are many other ways to prepare fish for the table. They can be used in soups, stews or gumbos. They can be pickled; flaked and used in cold salads; stuffed; served in casseroles; or embellished with a wide variety of sauces and garnishes.

Dozens of excellent fish cookbooks are available for anglers who would like to try more involved recipes.

Overall, fish are good for an angler's body and soul. They are truly a health food, and they are great fun to catch and prepare. That's why anglers who don't cook their catch should learn to do so. Through cooking and sharing your fish dishes with others, you get to enjoy them twice – once when caught, and once when served up as a gift to your friends.

CHAPTER 11

What to Try When Fish Aren't Biting

Every fisherman has those days when the fish just won't bite! You try your best places and baits and techniques, but you still can't get a nibble. It's like the fish don't exist. So, what do you do? Give up and go home?

Hardly! No question, on some days fish are less active and more difficult to get to bite. But there are still tricks to try to get some action. Feeding patterns change from day to day, or even hour to hour. One thing is for sure. If you give up and go home, you're certain not to catch anything. But if you stay and keep experimenting with different baits and tech-

Sky condition and water color can have a definite effect on fish location. If the sun is bright and the water is clear, most fish will hold on the shady side of trees, stumps, and bushes.

niques, you've still got a chance of hitting on the "magic combination" and making a good catch.

I've had days when action was painfully slow, then suddenly I'd hit on the right bait or spot or technique, and I'd make a good catch. I've also had the opposite to happen. Fish would be "jumping in the boat," then suddenly the bites stopped coming, like a light being turned off. Due to some change in the fish's mood, in the water conditions or whatever, the fish went from very active to inactive in a few minutes. Perhaps they just finished their meal and took a snooze?

Even when fish aren't actively feeding, I believe there are usually a few around that will still bite. It's like a fraternity house. Right after mealtime, somebody's snacking on leftovers. If you keep looking for fish, you can usually find a few hungry ones. Also, oftentimes you'll learn more about fishing when action is slow than when they're attacking the bait.

The point is, if fish aren't biting, don't give up. Instead, start changing all the variables you can – places, baits, methods – and hopefully you'll hit upon the right combination. At least by adopting this approach, you've got a chance of being successful and adding to your fishing knowledge.

In this chapter we will look at different factors that cause fish to bite, or not to bite. I'll also provide several suggestions for changing your approach when the fish are playing hard to get.

Factors that Affect Fish Behavior

The fish's world is an ever-changing one. There's always something going on beneath the surface. Weather, water and food conditions are constantly shifting, and this has a strong effect on fish's mood and activity level. Some sets of conditions cause fish to feed. Others turn them off.

This is why fishermen must be alert to condition changes and versatile in terms of adapting to them. They must analyze conditions

Persistence goes a long way toward catching fish. If bites are slow in coming, don't give up. Instead, start changing all the variables you can and hopefully you'll find the right combination to make a catch like this.

when they get to their fishing spot and then make a logical decision about where fish are holding and what's the best bait and presentation to catch them. Veteran fishermen are good at this. They have a wealth of experience to draw on. It's more difficult for beginners who don't have this "data base," but they must start somewhere. As they gain in experience, they will add to their knowledge, and they will learn to make the right moves faster.

Meanwhile, following are factors that affect fish's activity (i.e., feeding) levels. These are general guidelines, because in fishing there are exceptions to every rule. Still, for most fish, most of the time, these rules will apply.

How Weather Affects Fish

Weather is one condition that affects every fishing trip. It may be hot or cold. It may be sunny or cloudy. It may be windy or calm. It may be dry or rainy. It may be a period of stable weather, or it may be a time of changing weather. Sometimes weather will help you (cause fish to bite better), and sometimes it will hurt you (cause fish to quit biting). Smart anglers know how to take advantage of

good weather conditions and work around unfavorable ones.

Fish are very sensitive to changes in weather, such as a sudden shower, a passing cold front, rising or falling barometer, shifting winds, etc. These are the things you must be alert to and figure into your fishing plan. Here is how fish react to specific weather stimuli.

AIR TEMPERATURE – Water temperature is mainly regulated by air temperature. The warmer the air temp, the warmer the water. Fish are cold-blooded creatures, so their metabolism (how fast they burn up their food) is controlled by water temperature. In warmer water, fish use up their food faster. This means they have to feed more often to "keep their furnace stoked." On the other hand, in cool or cold water fish's metabolism slows down, and they don't have to feed as often. This is why fish are usually more active in warm water than in cool or cold water. (One exception to this is when very warm water is cooled off by a rain or a quick drop in air temperature. In very warm water, fish sometimes slip into a semi-active state, but a sudden temperature drop – even a degree or two – can "jump-start" a feeding spree).

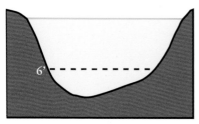

CLEAR WATER
Lure Disappears at 6 feet plus

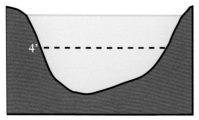

STAINED WATER
Lure Disappears at 2-6 feet

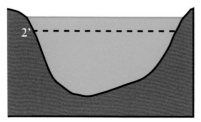

DARK WATER
Lure Disappears at 0-2 feet

Ethics & Etiquette

Crowd Fishing Ethics If you're fishing in a crowd (on the bank, fishing pier, tailwater, boat), avoid casting over another angler's line. If someone else hooks a fish, reel your line in so he can play the fish without tangling.

SKY CONDITION – Is the sky sunny or cloudy? Sky condition plays a big part in where fish are located. On cloudy days fish are more likely to be in shallow water and roaming around weeds, brush, docks, etc. But when bright sunshine penetrates the water (especially during midday), fish will usually retreat back into deeper water or shady areas (into the weeds or brush, beneath docks). Rarely do fish stay in shallow, open water during bright sunshine conditions.

PRECIPITATION – It's an old saying that fish bite better when it's raining. I think there is some truth in this if the rain is light to moderate, but not pouring. A light to moderate rain creates several positives: cloudy sky; surface disturbance; runoff washing new food into the water; new "color" from mud washing into the water; in hot weather, a sudden cooling of water temperature; a fresh infusion of oxygen into the water. All these things will stimulate fish to feed.

WIND – Wind may make fishing more difficult, but it also makes fish more likely to bite. Wind currents (waves) push baitfish into predictable feeding areas. Waves also stir up mud or silt along shoreline, adding color and dislodging craw-fish and other foods. Waves break up the surface and add oxygen to the water. Like rain, these are all things that cause fish to feed. This why it's usually better to fish the wind-exposed side of the lake as opposed to the sheltered side.

BAROMETRIC PRESSURE – Fish have a keen ability to determine changes in barometric pressure, and they respond to these changes by becoming more or less active. Fish are usually more active when the barometer is dropping, or when it's been high and steady for a couple of days. Fish are typically less active right after a sudden rise in barometric pressure.

One of the best times to go fishing is right before a storm or cold front passes. In these situations, the barometer may drop rapidly. Fish will sense this change, and sometimes they will go on a feeding binge. Conversely, after the front passes and the barometer heads back up, the fish usually quit feeding. Then, a day or two later when the barometer has stabilized, the fish will resume normal feeding patterns. However, by using techniques I will describe later in this chapter, you can still catch some fish on the heels of a cold front.

How Water Conditions Affect Fish

Water conditions frequently are tied to weather conditions. These include water temperature; water clarity (clear, dingy, muddy); water level (rising, falling, stable); amount of dissolved oxygen in the water; and currents. Following is how each of these conditions affects fish.

WATER TEMPERATURE – Fish seek areas where water temperature

If fish aren't biting what you're offering, change baits! Sometimes a simple lure switch is all that's needed to turn a slow-bite day into a good one. The only way you'll know is to try.

is most comfortable to them. This comfort zone varies from species to species. Warm water species (bass, crappie, sunfish, white bass, catfish) prefer a range of 70-85° F. Cool water species (walleye, pike, perch, muskies) like a range of 60-70° F. Cold water species (trout, salmon) prefer a range of 50-60° F.

Note that these ranges are preferences. Depending on time of year and prevailing water temperatures, fish are often found in water that's outside their preferred zone. However, they're usually more active – and bite better – when they're in their preferred range.

In many lakes and reservoirs, water temperature will change from the surface down to the depths. Water temperature near the surface changes faster than deeper water. Surface water warms faster in the day and cools off faster at night.

So, how does this help you find and catch fish? Say you're a bass fisherman on a lake in the middle of summer. The local fishing report gives the surface temperature at 80° F. You would expect most fish to be in deep water or in heavy, shady cover, since these areas would be cooler and more to the fish's liking. But at night, as the surface temperature cools off, bass might move up shallow where they'd be more accessible to anglers. In this case, night fishing might be more productive than daytime fishing.

On the other hand, in early spring, water surface temperature might be 55° F at dawn, but on a sunny day it might warm into the 60° F range by mid-day. In this case, the bass would be more active during this warmer period. Then their activity level would drop off as the water cools at dusk.

Many expert anglers use thermometers to check water temperature. As a beginner, you probably shouldn't worry about this until you gain more experience. But you should be aware that water temperature plays an important role in where fish are and how active they'll be. You can usually find water temperature for local waters in the newspaper, at the bait store, etc. These should be used as an overall guide. Actual water temperature in different areas of the lake may vary several degrees on the same day, due to depth, wind, water color, air temperature, current and other factors.

WATER CLARITY –When fishermen talk about water color, they mean water clarity. Some lakes,

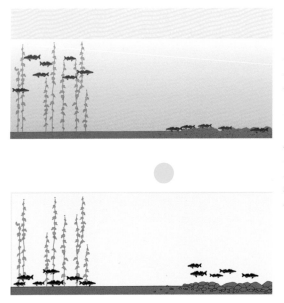

Light plays a key role in fish location. In overcast conditions (above) fish are likely to move into shallow water and move around in weeds, brush. Occasionally they will remain inactive near the bottom. In bright, sunny conditions (above, bottom) light penetrates the water and fish will usually retreat into deeper water or shade.

reservoirs and streams are clear with good underwater visibility; others are dingy, and still others are muddy. Also, water clarity changes frequently when it rains (washes mud into the lake) or when strong winds stir up mud along shore.

In clear water, fish usually hold deeper or tighter to brush, docks, rocks, etc. than fish in dingy or muddy water. This is because when visibility is better, fish are more vulnerable to predators, so they're spookier and tend to stay hidden in deep water or cover. In dingy or muddy water, they're hidden by the water color, so they can stay shallower, and they feel safer when roaming out away from cover.

As a rule of thumb, the best water to fish is slightly to moderately dingy. The fish will be shallower and not so spooky, yet there's enough visibility for them to see to feed. Many pro anglers start their day on a clear water lake or reservoir by searching for an area that "has some color." Again, these could be places where fresh water is running into the lake or where waves are pounding on the shoreline.

Extremely muddy water is not good, however, since it hampers a fish's ability to locate food (and baits)! Only scent-feeding species like catfish and bullheads are active in really muddy water.

WATER LEVEL – Water levels in lakes, reservoirs and rivers may rise or fall, depending on rain, water discharges from dams, or seasonal fluctuations. As a general rule, fish "follow a rise" (i.e., go shallow when the water is rising), then they move out deeper when the water level is falling.

In lakes and reservoirs, rising water makes fresh food available, and the bite is normally good in freshly flooded areas. Also, in rivers and streams, rising water and stronger currents wash new food downstream, and again, fish actively feed in this situation.

Falling water levels have just the opposite effect. Fish pull back into or near deep areas. If the water drop is gradual, they may continue to feed normally. But if the drop is fast, they will normally quit feeding until the water level stabilizes.

CURRENT – Again, a good way to think of current is "liquid wind." Current pushes food in the direction it's moving. Predator fish know this, and they rely on current to carry food to them.

Currents in rivers and streams are continuous, though they may increase or decrease depending on water flow. (After a heavy rain, current increases.) On the other hand, currents in tailwaters and power generation reservoirs are variable, depending on generation schedules. Currents may be slack, then the generators will turn on, and currents will suddenly be strong. When this happens, fish usually get very active, since moving water means better feeding conditions.

Another type current is "wind current." A prevailing wind will push water onto shore or through a narrow area between two points or islands. When this happens, fish move into these areas to feed. This is why fishing on the downwind shoreline is frequently better than on the upwind shoreline. Veteran anglers know that many times, fishing in windy areas is better than in calm areas.

Tricks to Try for Inactive Fish

All the above information helps you understand why fish sometimes bite, and why they sometimes don't. You also have an idea about fish locations during varying weather and water conditions. So, let's go back to the original

Many media fishing forecasts list "best feeding times" or "solunar periods." These are calculated according to when the moon exerts tidal pull.

Here's the theory. The moon's pull causes tides in the oceans, and saltwater anglers know that when the tide is running, the fishing is better. The same thing happens on freshwater lakes and reservoirs, but on a much smaller scale. Many experts believe that these gravity changes influence feeding behavior. The charts usually list two "major feeding periods" and two "minor feeding periods" each day.

Many anglers swear by these feeding times, while others ignore them. I think they have some merit, but I believe "moon times" may be secondary to other factors in determining whether fish will bite. I think fish feed better during major and minor periods than they do between these periods.

Fishing records also show that during the four-day period around the full moon, big fish are definitely more active. The four-day period around the new moon is the second best time to catch big fish. The days of the month between the full and new moons are the least productive.

How do I use this information? I still fish just as hard between feeding periods. But say I've got one spot I'm really counting on. I might plan to be at that location during a major feeding period. If I can fish only a couple of times a month, I'll try to go during the full or new moon.

question. What should you do when you can't get fish to bite?

CHANGE YOUR PRESENTATION – Try to figure out why the fish aren't biting and what it'll take to get them to hit. Then start experimenting with different locations, baits and retrieves. Here are suggestions for things to try.

CHANGE LOCATIONS – If you're not catching fish in one spot, try somewhere else. And, try a different type spot, not one just like the spot that just failed to produce. If you've been fishing in open water, try around cover. If you've been fishing around cover, try in the cover. If you've been fishing in shallow water, fish deeper. Remember that inactive fish like to hold in thick cover or deeper water. Choose your fishing location to match weather and water conditions.

CHANGE BAITS – If you've been fishing with artificial lures, switch to live bait. Or, if live bait isn't available, change to a lure that has a more subtle action. Also, change to a smaller lure. Inactive fish are more likely to take a small, slow-moving bait than a big, active one.

Many years ago Charlie Brewer of the Slider Lure Company told me a story that makes this point. He said to imagine that I'd just eaten a steak dinner, and I'd settled into an easy chair for a nap (i.e., I'm inactive). If somebody brought me another steak, I'd refuse it. But if that person passed a small dish of ice cream under my nose, I might take a bite. Charlie said it's the same with fish. After a feeding spree, they rest. If a large bait swims by, they'll probably ignore it. But if a small "dessert bait" glides right under their nose, they might suck it in.

SLOW THE RETRIEVE – This goes hand-in-hand with Charlie's "dessert bait" theory. Active fish will attack a fast-moving lure. But when feeding is over, they're no longer in a "chase mode." They'll ignore speedy lures. However, if a slow, lazy bait comes drifting or hopping along, and they don't have to chase it down to catch it, they might still bite it.

CHANGE LURE COLORS – As I stated in a previous chapter, I believe lure colors is one of the least important factors in whether or not fish will bite. Still, sometimes changing lure color will make a difference. The only way to find out is to try another color.

SWITCH TO LIGHTER LINE – Lighter line is harder for spooky fish to see. Lighter line also allows you to cast smaller, more subtle baits and to work these baits with a freer, more lifelike action. (Switching to lighter line might be impractical when using a spincast or casting reel. But with a spinning

When bites are hard to come by, down-sizing baits is a good way to coax fish into biting. A small plastic worm fished with a slow, subtle action is an effective combination for catching inactive bass.

What to Try When Fish Aren't Biting 187

Especially in summer, fish bite better at dawn and dusk, when temperatures are cooler and sunlight is dim. Anglers can maximize their odds of catching fish by fishing during peak activity times.

reel, all you have to do is change spools. It takes less than a minute to change spools and retie a lure.) **BE MORE CAREFUL IN YOUR APPROACH** – Sometimes simple carelessness on your part is why fish don't bite. Don't let them see you. Don't get too close to them. Don't bang on the boat. Don't cast a lure or bait directly on top of them. Instead, cast past where you think they're holding (log, weeds, brush, etc.), then reel the bait into them. Overall, be alert to and avoid things that might tip fish off as to your presence.

FISH AT A DIFFERENT TIME – This may be the best tip of all. If you're fishing in the middle of a bright summer day, you're a lot more likely to catch fish at dawn, dusk or night. Come back when the fish are more likely to be feeding.

Also, watch the weather and try to anticipate feeding sprees. We know that fish bite better when it's cloudy, especially right before a front passes. If you go fishing when fish are more likely to bite, you increase your chances of catching them.

TRY FOR ANOTHER SPECIES – If the bass aren't biting, try for bluegill. Don't be "species stubborn." Sometimes one species will be more active or available than another. Don't be reluctant to switch to another type fishing. As I've said before, catching anything is preferable to getting skunked.

Summary

SUCCESS IN FISHING – like any other sport – comes from building on fundamentals. We laid our "foundation" for fishing in earlier chapters. Now, in this chapter, we've introduced a new and advanced plateau of fishing knowledge. By understanding how fish react to different stimuli, and by figuring these reactions into your fishing strategy, you're refining those fundamentals. And the more you refine, the better angler you'll be.

The best way to learn these fundamentals is to simply go fishing as often as possible and gain as much experience as you can. Try new things. Put the information in this chapter to the test. Then your skills will increase, and you'll catch fish more often than before. For my money, being skillful is far better than being lucky. Being skillful is what it takes to get reluctant fish to bite!

CHAPTER 12

Boats, Motors, and Boating Accessories

I learned to fish as a small boy on the back seat of my dad's homemade johnboat. There was nothing fancy about it, but fancy doesn't have much to do with success. Dad's little boat got us on the water and took us to the holes where crappie lived. I remember days when we completely filled our cooler and had "extras" scattered along the boat's floor.

An aluminum johnboat is a wise choice for beginning anglers who spend most of their fishing time on small waters. These boats are economical, portable and stable enough to provide a good casting platform.

Not many beginners will enjoy the same learning opportunities. Most will start fishing from the bank, bridge or dock. But sooner or later, as your skills increase, you'll want to broaden your horizons and get out "on the water."

It's not that you can't catch fish around the banks. You certainly can, as we've noted in previous chapters. However, having a boat or some floating platform allows you to step up to another level in fishing. It opens a whole new world, allowing you to cover more water and be more versatile in your overall approach to the sport. In other words, a boat expands your fishing opportunities, and it allows you to increase your knowledge and fun.

Types of Boats

Fishing boats come in a broad range of designs and prices. High end bass boats cost in the mid-$30,000 range! On the low end are float tubes that start around $50. The expensive rigs are highly technical and ultimately functional, and someday you might decide to purchase one. But with this book's theme of keeping fishing simple, we'll stick to the fundamental, less expensive, easier-to-maintain

models that beginning anglers are more likely to buy. These include johnboats, V-hulls, canoes, "bass buggies," inflatables and, again, float tubes.

Following are looks at each of these types of boats, the waters where they work best, and their advantages and disadvantages.

Johnboats

The aluminum johnboat may be the best all-purpose fishing boat for beginners. Johnboats have a flat bottom and a square or semi- V bow design. They are very stable and draw only a few inches of water, which enables them to traverse shallow areas. Johnboats were designed for streams, but a deep-sided, wide-beamed johnboat also adapts well to large open lakes. These boats perform well with outboard motors.

Top-of-the-line bass boats are super fishing machines. They feature powerful outboards, a range of electronics, and the size and stability needed to fish big water.

Johnboats come in a range of lengths, from 8 to more than 20 feet. However, the 12- and 14-foot models are most popular. These are light enough to be cartopped and carried to the water by two anglers. This means you can use a johnboat wherever you can drive close to a stream, pond bank or lakeshore.

Johnboats have three minor disadvantages: the flat hull provides a rough ride in choppy water; johnboats are clumsy to paddle; because of their allmetal construction, they are noisy when objects are dropped or banged against the sides.

But all in all, johnboats make very practical, relatively inexpensive fishing boats for beginners. Many anglers buy basic johnboats and customize them with seats, live well, carpet, rod holders, etc.

V-Hull

The V-hull is the workhorse of fishing boats. It's called "Vhull" because it has a V-shaped bow that tapers back to a flatbottomed hull. This allows the V-hull to slice through waves, giving a smoother, safer ride in rough water.

Most are made of fiberglass or aluminum. Heavier fiberglass boats provide a smoother ride in choppy water. Most popular Vhull sizes are 12-18 feet. These boats are normally fitted with mid-sized outboards (25-100 horsepower).

A disadvantage of the V-hull is it's weight. Larger V-hulls require trailers, and must be launched from ramps. They are awkward to paddle, but maneuver well with an electric motor.

These boats are the standard on big lakes and rivers because of their ability to handle rough water. As with johnboats, they are often customized with a broad range of accessories. Some models are equipped with console steering. Boat dealers sell a range of models, from basic nofrills boats to those with motor and accessories factory-installed. V-hulls are typically more expensive than johnboats.

Canoes

Canoes suffer from bad PR. Inexperienced canoeists believe these boats are too tippy for fishing. The truth is, certain models are very stable, and make excellent fishing boats for a wide range of waters. With only a little practice, beginners can handle a canoe and fish confidently from it.

Canoes offer anglers several advantages. They are relatively

Canoes are inexpensive, portable and easy to learn to paddle. All these features make a canoe a good choice for fishing on flowing waters or small ponds and lakes.

inexpensive and are extremely portable. They can be car-topped and carried to lakes or streams far off the beaten path. They are also ideal for small, urban waters where bigger boats are impractical or even disallowed. Canoes draw only inches of water. They are highly maneuverable and can be paddled through shallow riffles or bays. Also, some models can be outfitted with small outboards or electric motors for motorized running.

Canoes are made from several materials: fiberglass, aluminum, polyethylene. They come in square stern and double-end models. (Square stern canoes are best for using outboards or electric motors. Small motors may also be used on double-end canoes with a side-mount bracket near the stern.)

Fishermen shopping for a canoe should strongly consider a 16- or 17-foot model that has a wide beam and a flat bottom. This offers the greatest stability and versatility.

"Bass Buggies"

This type boat is also known as a mini-bass boat, but can be used for many different species. It is a rectangular, hard plastic casting platform supported by flotation arms running beneath both sides. Bass buggies come in one and two-man models, ranging up to 10 feet in length. Most have molded-in seats, rod wells, battery compartments, etc. Most use an electric trolling motor but a few larger models accept a small outboard motor.

Bass buggies are mainly used on small, protected waters such as ponds, sloughs, strip mine pits and arms of larger lakes. They are highly maneuverable in standing timber, brush and other cover. They float in only a few inches of water. Bass buggies should not be used on large lakes or rivers with high waves or strong current.

Bass buggies are bulky, which means they aren't very portable. They must be hauled in a pickup bed or on a small trailer.

Inflatables

Inflatables are like rubber rafts, except today these "blow-up" boats are mostly made from PVC plastic. They come in a variety of sizes and shapes. The smallest models accommodate one passenger while the largest carry six people or more. These boats can be carried in a car trunk or SUV,

backpacked to out-of-the-way waters and inflated on the spot. Portability is an inflatable boat's strongest advantage.

Inflatables have several disadvantages, however. They are more a means of water transportation than a true fishing boat. Their soft sides and bottom make them unstable for stand-up casting. Inflatables are subject to puncture from sharp objects, though most are constructed with separate flotation panels, so a puncture in one compartment won't sink the boat. Also, most inflatables come with easy-to-use repair kits. These boats are unwieldy to paddle, but some have a special motor-mount bracket that allows use of an electric motor or small outboard. One of the most attractive features of inflatables is price. They are very inexpensive. Two-man models start at around $50.

Float Tubes

The float tube (also called a "belly boat") isn't a standard boat like the others mentioned in this chapter. The float tube is a floating doughnut with a sewn-in seat and leg holes. An angler carries it to his fishing site, steps in, pulls it up around his waist, then walks into

The V-hull is the workhorse of fishing boats. It's called "V-hull" because it has a V-shaped bow that tapers back to a flat hull. The V-hull is designed to slice through waves and provide a safe, dry ride in rough water.

the water. When he's deep enough for the float tube to support his weight, he propels himself by kicking with swim fins or special paddles attached to his boots. (Most float tube anglers wear waders, though they're not necessary if the water is warm.)

Float tubes are used to fish close to shore in small, quiet waters. They've very maneuverable, but they're slow. They're good for fishing in flooded brush, timber, patches of reeds or cattails or other similar spots that are difficult to reach by boat. Also, since float tubes are very quiet, they're good for slipping up on spooky fish.

Float tubes should not be used in strong-wind/open-lake situations. High waves can flip you upside down, and float tubes can be difficult to right. Again, these "boats" should be confined to quiet, close-to-shore fishing.

Float tubes are highly portable and fairly inexpensive. They come in basic or deluxe models. Deluxe models come with such features as zippered tackle holders, shoulder straps, an inflatable backrest and Velcro rod holders.

Motors

Motors aren't absolutely necessary for fishing, but in many cases they certainly make the job easier. You must decide if you need a motor by the type boat you have and the water where you plan to fish. If you'll be using a small boat on remote streams, small ponds or lakes, paddles may be all the power you need. But if you'll be on larger waters where you'll have to cover more distance, or where winds or currents can be strong, a larger boat with a motor will be more practical and efficient.

Fishing motors come in two varieties: outboard and electric. Outboard (gas-powered) motors are more powerful and are used mainly for running long distances – getting from one spot to the next. Electric (battery-powered) motors are less powerful and much quieter. Their job is to ease the boat through the target area while the angler fishes. Electric motors are also used as the main power source on waters where outboards aren't allowed.

Outboard Motors

New outboard motors are expensive. Often they cost more than the boat they power. But anglers should view an outboard as a long-term investment. Modern outboards are dependable and easy to

operate and will last many years if properly maintained.

Outboards range from 1.5 to 250-plus horsepower. Smaller motors are lightweight and portable. They attach to the boat's stern with clamp mounts. Larger motors are heavy, and they're permanently bolted onto the stern.

The main consideration when buying a motor is not to overpower the boat. All boats list maximum horsepower ratings either on the stern plate or in the owner's instructions. Never exceed these ratings — overpowered boats are unsafe to operate.

Electric Motors

Most electric motors fall into one of two categories: 12-volt and 24-volt. Twelve-volt motors are powered by one 12-volt battery. Twenty-four volt motors require two linked 12-volt batteries. The obvious difference between the two is available power, which is measured in "pounds of thrust." The 24-volt motor is much stronger than a 12-volt. Twenty-four volt motors are normally used on big boats that operate in rough water. On smaller boats and quiet waters, a 12-volt motor is adequate.

Electric motors have different types of mounts and methods

Buying Your Fishing Rig

It's obvious now that, even with a simple fishing rig, you're looking at a sizeable investment. When it's time to go shopping, check around for a package deal. By buying a boat, motor, trailer, fish locater and accessories from one dealer, you have a better bargaining position for a discount.

Do your homework. Don't buy a rig without shopping around. Ask dealers for advice on what boat, motor, and accessories you'll need for where you'll be fishing. Check prices, collect literature, study it and decide for sure what you want before making any purchase commitment.

Boat dealers generally offer their best deals in late summer or fall, toward the end of the fishing season. At this time you're in a better position to bargain and wait for them to come down on price. Don't be in a hurry to buy your fishing rig. This is a big step, and you should proceed slowly and carefully.

Once you do take the step, however, you'll have graduated up to fishing's "high school." You'll have access to your chosen lake, river or stream's entire angling menu. No longer will you have to fish from shore and watch the boats go by. Now you can join them. The door will suddenly open to many new fishing challenges and experiences, more than you can experience in a lifetime.

of operation. Some motors have "clamp-on" mounts with screws to tighten down on the sides or transom of the boat. Others have bow mounts that attach permanently to the front of the boat. Some electric motors are operated by hand, while others have foot controls that allow the user to run the motor while keeping his hands free to fish. Remote- and radio-control electric motors are available. Microchip technology is being used to upgrade electric motors each year, making them ever more "user friendly."

It is much more efficient for an electric motor to pull a boat rather than push it. A boat with an electric motor mounted on or near the bow is easier to propel and steer than one with an electric motor on the transom.

When shopping for an electric motor, you'll find models with many options and power ratings. My recommendation for a beginner's first electric is a 12-volt clamp-on model with 20-40 pounds of thrust. Remember that the heavier your boat, the more power you'll need to pull or push it. Also, electric motor shafts come in different lengths. Owners of johnboats, canoes and bass

Outboard motors come in a wide range of horsepower sizes. Modern outboards are expensive, but they are good investments. They will last for years if properly maintained.

A clamp-on electric motor is a good choice for powering a smaller johnboat, V-hull or bass buggie. They are quiet so they won't scare fish, yet they are strong enough to maneuver a boat into the best casting position.

buggies will probably need motors with shafts that are 30 or 36 inches long. Owners of Vhulls may need a motor with a 42-inch shaft, since these boats have higher sides and are more likely to be used in rolling waves. Boat dealers can provide guidelines for choosing the right shaft length.

Fish Locaters

A fish locater is an angler's "eyes under the water." Its basic function is to show the bottom and objects between the surface and the bottom. Knowing water depth is important both from a safety standpoint and also for fishing efficiency. Fish locaters can show submerged structure: drop-offs, sunken channels, stumps, brush, rocks, weeds, etc. A good fish locater can even tell whether the bottom is soft or hard, and can pinpoint concentrations of bait- and gamefish.

Even though a fish finder is fairly expensive (starting at around $75), it is considered an almost indispensable tool by serious anglers. I recommend one for all beginners who will be fishing away from shore on lakes and large rivers. A fish locater, properly used will pay great dividends in terms of numbers of fish caught.

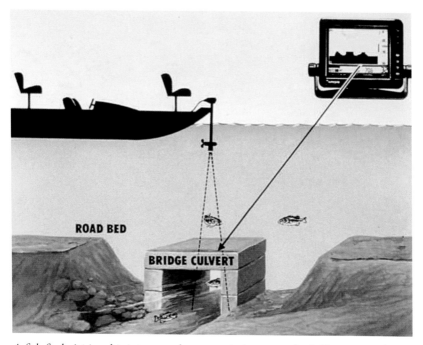

A fish finder's signal is interpreted as a grapic image on the LCD screen. The computer uses the transponders signal to "paint" a picture of the bottom, features, and hanging fish.

A fish locater is a sonar unit that sends out sound waves that strike underwater objects. Then the fish locater measures how long it takes the echoes to bounce back to the sending unit. The deeper an object in the water, the longer the time required for this roundtrip. The fish locater then translates this time into a distance display, showing bottom depth and objects between the surface and bottom.

Most modern fish locaters are LCD units ("liquid crystal display") that actually draw chart-like pictures of what's beneath the boat. The latest technology includes different colors in this display to help users distinguish between fish and other underwater features. You can actually see fish you're trying to catch!

Boat Accessories

The boat, motor and fish locater make up the core of the fishing rig, but several other accessories are needed to complete the package.

A fish locater uses sonar to indicate depth and the location of underwater structure. An angler can analyze a body of water and discover the best fishing locations.

State and federal laws require certain safety equipment on all boats. Boats under 16 feet must carry a Coast Guard-approved flotation device for each passenger, paddle, some type of sound signal (whistle, air horn, etc.), running lights if the boat is to be used at night, and a fire extinguisher if gas is kept in an enclosed compartment. Boats 16 feet and longer must meet these requirements, plus the flotation devices must be wearable life preservers, and the boat must also have a throwable flotation device (cushion, safety ring, etc). For a full review of these requirements, contact your state water safety office.

Beyond these required items, you may consider a broad array of boat accessories: batteries and battery boxes, battery charger, landing net, anchor and rope, seats, fish basket, bilge pump, rod holders and marker floats. These and other accessories will complete

Most bass boats use a stern mounted, gasoline powered outboard motor for travelling on lakes and rivers and an electric trolling motor, mounted near the bow, to maneuver around fishing spots.

your boat package and make your fishing easier.

There are two types of marine batteries: "deep cycle" and "quick start." Deep-cycle batteries release small amounts of electricity over extended time periods. They are used primarily to power electric motors. Quick-start batteries provide short, powerful bursts of electricity. They are intended for starting outboards and also for running electric accessories other than the electric motor.

Remember four tips for battery maintenance. First, always recharge your batteries immediately after use. Don't allow them to sit discharged for long periods. Second, if your battery is not sealed – you can open the cell caps to check solution levels. Keep solution at recommended levels. Third, don't overcharge your batteries. If your batteries don't have charge indicators, use a hydrometer and check charge level as you recharge. Quit charging when the hydrometer reads "full charge." And fourth, during winter, charge batteries fully, then store them in a cool, dry place.

CHAPTER 13

Increasing Your
Fishing Skills

Several years ago I fished the fabled Manistee River in north-central Michigan, one of the very best brown and brook trout streams in the Midwest. My host was a local guide who knew all the tricks for catching these fish, even when conditions were tough and they didn't want to bite. We had chosen one of those days!

One of the best ways to learn more about fishing is to hire a guide for a day of on-water instruction. Go with the objective of learning about fishing, and don't be afraid to ask your guide questions about his methods.

We were fly-fishing, and our delicate dry flies had tempted only a few small brookies. The bigger browns were no-shows!

My guide wasn't to be denied. When our dry fly presentation failed to produce, he started poking around in his fly-box, and he came out with an ugly looking wet fly called the Skunk. After tying it on, he started picking up brown trout by casting it upstream of deep holes and root wads and allowing the fly to sink down to where the fish were sulking.

It didn't take long for me to bum a Skunk off my teacher and start copying his "dead drift" method of offering it to the trout. Regardless of its ugly appearance, this fly was the perfect imitation of "dinner" served to the fish, and it changed a slow day into one I remember now for its fast action and "tempestuous trout."

What's the lesson here? When it comes to fishing, you'll never know everything! You'll never be too smart to pick up new information or tricks that'll help you catch more fish, regardless of species. Savvy fishermen are those who continually add to their knowledge and skills, who master new techniques, and who dare to try new waters and species. Learning to fish should be a never-ending process for both beginners and experts. Beginners just have more to learn.

After you've mastered the basics, it's time to expand your knowledge of fishing. The following instructions will serve as a guideline to help you do this.

Practice Makes Perfect… Almost!

Anglers are athletes, even though their sport doesn't demand the strength of football players or the stamina of long-distance runners. Fishing requires a unique combination of mental and physical skills, plus a measure of finesse. One common thread binds fishermen with other athletes: the more they practice, the better they become. If you fish a dozen times a year, you'll be better than if you fish only twice.

Fishing practice does two things. First, it increases your mental sharpness. You learn from your mistakes, which are inevitible. Practicing allows you to experiment with different baits and techniques, to build an inventory of spots, baits and methods that have produced fish in the past. In essence, frequent fishing trips build a storehouse of experience from which to draw when presented with new or different situations.

Second, practice develops the physical coordination and "feel" you need to be an effective angler. You'll learn to be more comfortable with your tackle and more able to tell when you're getting a bite. You'll also know when to set the hook, and you'll be more in tune with the total fishing environment. This all combines to improve your consistency in making good catches.

Casting Practice

Over the years I've fished with many of North America's top fishing pros, and I've asked them, "What do average anglers need to work on most?" Most have answered, "Casting accuracy." In many fishing situations, getting a bite depends on being able to drop a lure or bait in exactly the right spot – not two feet to the side, back or front.

That's why beginning fishermen should work at learning to cast accurately. You can do this in spare time by practice-casting in your backyard. Set up a target – bucket, garbage can top, etc. Next, tie a practice plug onto the end of your line. (A practice plug is a plastic, teardrop-shaped weight with no hooks.) Back away from your target and cast to it, over and over. When you're able to hit the target consistently, move back to 15 yards, then 20, then 25.

Begin casting by holding your rod in front of your nose. Line it up with your target, and make your cast. When you're comfortable with this style, add sidearm and backhand casting. Sometimes you'll need to make such close-to-the-water casts to get your lure under boat docks, overhanging limbs and other similar spots where fish might be hiding.

Practice casting frequently, but keep sessions short – approximately 15 minutes. Concentrate on making smooth casts, allowing rod action to propel the plug. Don't overpower it. Accurate casting is a matter of easy coordination rather than strength.

Attend Fishing Seminars

Fishing seminars are held throughout the country, usually in late winter or early spring. Most seminars are either small, informal gatherings in tackle shops, or large formal affairs at sport shows, large retail stores, colleges or similar sites. Some are free-of-charge, while others charge an entry fee. These seminars feature experts who can give you pointers on local fishing. When you attend, take notes, ask questions, collect available literature, and analyze how the tips apply to your fishing spots and methods. Watch for seminar notices in tackle stores, on your newspaper's outdoor page, and in magazines and other advertising outlets.

Fish with a Guide

Another way to add to your fishing knowledge is to take lessons from a pro. Golfers, tennis players and other athletes take lessons, and anglers should consider doing likewise.

The way to take lessons in fishing is to hire a guide for a day of on-the-water instruction. This is better, though more expensive, than attending seminars. In this case, the "classroom" is a lake or river, and you get to learn "hands-on." A guide will answer your questions and show you proven spots and techniques. Overall, this one-on-one session can be the greatest shortcut to fishing success that you will ever take.

Hiring a professional guide will run $100-250 per day. If this is too expensive, consider hiring him for half a day or finding a partner to split the cost.

Go with the objective of learning about fishing. Ask your guide how he finds fish, why he fishes the way he does, and what tips are most important. You've employed a tutor, and it's up to you to learn as much as you can from him. If you catch fish and have fun, that's a bonus. But your main focus should be to gain as much practical fishing information as possible.

Fish in a Tournament

You can also get on-the-water instruction by entering a fishing tournament. (Some tournaments require participants to meet age restrictions – typically over 16 years.) Specifically, I'm referring to "draw" tournaments where contestants are paired by random drawing. In this case, your tournament entry fee is similar to money paid for a guide. It's your cost for sharing the boat and observing an experienced angler performing at his best.

There are risks in this. You're taking a chance that you may not draw a good partner, though most tournament contestants will be seasoned veterans. You won't be able to quiz your partner like you would a guide. (He will be concentrating on his fishing and

Attending a fishing tournament – as a contestant or a spectator – is a good way to improve your fishing skills. As a contestant, you'll get to watch an expert go about his business on the water. Even by going to a weigh-in you can learn by listening to anglers describe techniques they used to catch their fish.

not wanting to be distracted by your questions.) But you'll be able to study how he fishes, and most partners won't mind offering an explanation of what they're doing.

If the idea of entering a tournament appeals to you, don't be shy about following through. Just explain to your partner that you've entered as a learning experience, and you're willing to try whatever tournament tactics he wishes. Chances are, he'll be happy not to draw a partner who wants to go somewhere else or veer from his fishing strategy.

Books, Magazines, Videos, Fishing Websites

Anglers who want to increase their knowledge of fishing can buy, subscribe to, rent, borrow or log onto instructional books, magazines, videos or websites. Many of these are too technical to benefit beginners. But hopefully you are now beyond the novice stage, and you've progressed to where you can learn and benefit from these teaching aids.

You can be selective because there are so many different books, magazines, videos and websites available. There are publications, videos and sites specifically about fishing for bass, crappie, trout, etc. Choose those which offer details about catching fish you've selected as your target species and that are most relevant to the waters you fish. Also, it's possible to find on-line fishing friends with whom you can chat and ask questions.

Don't overlook your public library. All libraries have fishing books and a variety of fishing and outdoor magazines. Most also have PCs with internet access available to the public.

Join a Fishing Club

Many towns and cities have fishing clubs, and most welcome new members. By joining, you'll make new friends who share your interest in fishing, and you can learn a lot from other members. If you don't know how to contact a local fishing club, call your newspaper's outdoor writer, your game warden or tackle store, and ask how to get in touch with club members.

Keeping a Fishing Log

To beginners, fishing may seem like an ever-changing sport. Fish move from place to place. They prefer different foods at different times.

Practice might not make an angler perfect, but it will certainly improve his skills. The more an angler fishes, the better he will become at such things as reading water, casting, detecting bites, playing fish, etc.

One day they're active and biting anything that moves. The next day they're inactive, and they refuse the most tempting baits.

Over the years, though, you'll learn that fish follow definite patterns, and catching them does likewise. At a certain time of year, under certain combinations of weather and water conditions, fish will be very predictable in terms of location, lure preference, etc.

Anglers learn to recognize these patterns and predict fish behavior in two ways: through years

Even little fish can produce big thrills, and anglers who can cast well will catch more fish – period! Being able to toss a lure into tight spots where fish are hiding is very important. Anglers should practice casting in the backyard to improve their ability to do this.

of fishing experience and making mental notes; or by keeping a written log and referring to it before each new outing.

The written method is more reliable than memory, and it's a faster way for beginning fishermen to put together a body of facts for future reference. I recommend that all fishermen maintain a log and update it after each fishing trip. Some tackle stores and mail-order retailers sell fishing logs, or you can keep your own on a personal computer. Record dates; locations; weather and water conditions;

methods, baits and tackle used; fish caught; and other details.

If you have a favorite body of water, keep updated on it with a map showing the location of fish caught by yourself and others. As the seasons pass, you'll soon realize locations where fish are caught and also where successful anglers fish.

Keeping a log takes effort, but it will help you recognize patterns for choosing the right spots and methods. Also, in years to come, a log will rekindle warm memories of enjoyable trips in the past.

CHAPTER 14

Safety In Fishing

Several years ago I had one of my worst scares ever while fishing on my home lake. I was in my boat alone, casting for bass around a shoreline on the far side of the lake. I'd noticed storm clouds building to the west, and I'd heard thunder rumbling. But the fish were biting, and I allowed the excitement of the moment to overrule my good sense to get back to the boat ramp before the storm broke.

When I finally decided to head back in, I'd waited too long. When I was in the middle of the lake, a fierce wind struck, and it seemed as though my small boat and I were in the North Atlantic. Waves were as high as my head. Spray drenched me, and the boat started taking water.

Winter fishermen should be prepared with gloves, face mask and good boots and socks. Anglers must be prepared for two special perils that this season brings. One is hypothermia – a lowering of the body's core temperature through rapid heat loss. The second danger is frostbite.

I cinched my life vest up tight. My only hope of not swamping was to turn downwind and run with the waves. After an anxious 15-minute ride, I beached in a desolate cove, where I was stuck for a couple of hours while the storm passed. Rain poured down, and lightning popped! I sat huddled in a gully, soaked and miserable, but at least I was okay.

Overall, fishing is a very safe sport, but it does involve certain hazards. Some of these may be life-threatening, others only discomforting. The old adage "an ounce of prevention is worth a pound of cure" applies. If I'd started back to the boat ramp 15 minutes earlier, I wouldn't have wound up in such a predicament. If the angler down the lake had done the same, he'd probably be alive today!

Following is a look at safety considerations in fishing, at dangers which can arise and how to avoid or deal with them. We'll take them in order of seriousness: life-threatening first, then discomforting second.

Weather Perils of Fishing

LIGHTNING – Because fishing is an outdoor sport, you will experience different types of weather. This means that sooner or later you'll be exposed to one of the

Fishing has certain hazards. A combination of open water and high winds, can swamp a boat if resulting waves get too high. Anglers should always watch the weather and be careful to avoiding potential danger on the water.

most dangerous of all natural killers: lightning. Lightning doesn't get the scare publicity that tornadoes, hurricanes and other sensational weather phenomena do. But each year lightning claims more lives than all other weather-related accidents combined. Invariably, some of these victims are fishermen.

Kids learn at an early age that lightning strikes tall objects. Tallness is relative. A fisherman in a boat on a lake is tall in comparison to what's around him. The same is true about an angler standing on a flat, barren shoreline. In either case, if the fisherman is using a rod (particularly graphite), in effect he's holding a lightning rod, and he's inviting disaster.

The cardinal rule is never allow yourself to get caught where lightning is likely to strike. If you see a storm coming, get off the water or away from high areas or tall objects. The safest place to be is inside a house or vehicle. Don't stand under isolated trees or poles. If you get caught in an electrical storm, wait it out in the lowest spot you can find, and keep a low profile. If you get caught on the water and can't make it to shore, stow your rods and lie down in the boat.

HIGH WINDS – High winds are another weather peril for anglers in boats. Small boats and big waves are a bad combination. If you think the waves are too high, don't go out. If you are out and see a storm coming, head in. If you get caught in high waves and start taking water, forget about trying to get back to the dock or ramp. Turn and go with the wind. Let the waves take you where they may.

If you are in a boat that does swamp, stay in it rather than abandon it. Most boats today have level flotation, and even if they fill with water, they won't sink. Keep your life jacket cinched tightly, try to

A hook buried in a hand is a quick way to ruin a fishing trip. Sooner or later most anglers will be presented with this dilemma. They have the choice of going to a doctor to have it removed or removing it themselves by using the "yank" method described in this chapter.

stay calm, and wait for someone to come to your rescue.

FOG – Sometimes you may be tempted to head out onto a foggy lake. My advice is don't go. When you can't see where you're going, you risk running into an unseen object or getting lost. Stay at the boat ramp until the fog lifts. You won't miss much fishing time, and you won't be taking unnecessary chances.

Also, keep a GPS or a compass handy in case fog rolls in. I have a GPS on my fish finder, and I also keep a small compass in my tackle box. Fog causes you to lose all sense of direction, and a GPS or compass can help you find your way back to the launch site.

HYPOTHERMIA – "Exposure" is the common term for hypothermia. This is a loss of body heat – typically caused by getting wet -

that can eventually cause death. This is not just a winter problem. It can occur in other seasons, too. It's usually brought on by a combination of cool air, wind and wet clothes. Evaporation of moisture from clothing causes a rapid heat loss, and this leads to a drop in body temperature. If this drop is severe, death can follow.

The first sign of hypothermia is mild shivering. This is the body's way of trying to warm itself, and it's also a warning signal of trouble. If something isn't done to reverse this situation, the shivering can become uncontrollable, and the victim starts losing feeling in his arms and legs. His speech becomes slurred, and his thinking gets fuzzy. If his body temperature continues to drop (75-80° F), he will slip into a coma and possibly die.

If you or a fishing buddy starts shivering, don't ignore this signal! It's time to take action. There are two things to do: (1) remove the cause of cooling (wet clothing); and (2) restore body heat. This can be done by replacing wet clothes with dry ones (especially a dry cap or hat), by drinking warm fluids (coffee, tea, etc.), by eating energyrich foods (candy), and by warming next to a fire or some

Ethics & Etiquette

Ramp Courtesy When you're launching a boat, and other fishermen are waiting behind you, be ready when it's your turn on the ramp. Have all your gear in the boat and the tie-down straps undone. Do anything else you have to before getting to the ramp. When it's your turn to launch, you can do so quickly without keeping others waiting longer than necessary.

other heat source. You must stop the loss of body heat and restore it to a normal level. If the symptoms progress to uncontrollable shivering, get medical help fast. Remember, hypothermia is a killer.

FROSTBITE – Frostbite can be a threat to winter fishermen. In essence, this is a burn that occurs when skin is exposed to a combination of very cold air, moisture and wind. Circulation drops. The flesh becomes numb and freezes. Frostbitten toes or fingers turn white, and they're very cold to the touch.

Frostbite can be avoided by moving around, replacing wet gloves or socks with dry ones, holding numb fingers under your armpit, or holding a warm hand over an exposed ear, nose or cheek.

How to Remove Embedded Hooks

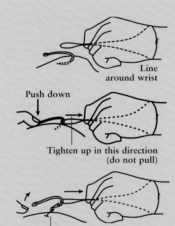

Line around wrist

Push down

Tighten up in this direction (do not pull)

Hook will pop up in this direction

You'll need two 18-inch pieces of strong twine. (Monofilament doubled over works well.) If the embedded hook is attached to a lure, remove the lure so only the hook remains. Run one piece of twine through the eye (hole) of the hook, and hold it snug against the skin. With the other hand, loop the other piece of twine through the bend of the hook (between the skin and the hook), pull out all slack, and get a strong grip. If you're doing this properly, the two pieces of string will be pulling in opposite directions.

Now, hold the hook eye firmly in place next to the skin. With the other string, yank up and away very suddenly and forcefully. Done properly, this yields a fulcrum movement that pops the barb back out the entry hole. Wash the puncture wound, treat it with antiseptic and apply a Band-Aid, then go back fishing. Watch closely the next few days for any sign of infection, and if any appears, seek medical attention.

Despite your best prevention efforts, sooner or later you or your fishing partner will likely be on the receiving end of a flying hook, or you'll sit or step on a hook. When this happens, you have a choice. You can go to a doctor and have it surgically removed, or you can pull the hook out yourself by the following method, which is simple and fairly painless.

If frostbite does occur, don't rub it. Instead, place the frostbitten area next to warm skin, and leave it there to thaw. Seek medical attention.

The Danger of Drowning

Drowning is a constant danger to fishermen. Each year we hear tragic stories of anglers who have fallen out of boats or off the bank and were lost. This danger is easily avoided. Following are commonsense rules for making sure you won't become a drowning victim.

WEAR A LIFE PRESERVER. – Using a life preserver is the "ounce of prevention" I mentioned earlier. Very few anglers drown while wearing a Coast Guard-approved personal flotation device (PFD). Whenever you're in a boat, you're required to have such a preserver with you. You're not required to wear it, however, and this gets many lackadaisical fishermen in trouble.

Accidents happen when you least expect them, and they happen quickly. If you're not wearing your life preserver, and your boat suddenly overturns, you probably won't have a chance to put your PFD on. Always wear your PFD when the boat is running, and zip it up or tie it. Also, it's a good idea to wear it even when the boat's not running, especially if you're a poor swimmer. A vesttype preserver isn't bulky. It's comfortable, and it won't interfere with your fishing.

Or, perhaps a better option is an approved inflatable-type PFD that's worn like suspenders. If you fall out of the boat, a quick tug on a lanyard activates a CO2 cartridge that instantly inflates the PFD.

Bank fishermen should also consider wearing a PFD. Especially if you're fishing along steep banks, tailraces, docks, bridges or similar spots. Children should never be allowed close to such spots without wearing a securely fastened PFD.

DON'T OVERLOAD THE BOAT. – One of the worst incidents in my life was watching a duck hunter drown. Four grown men and a retriever were in a small johnboat motoring across the lake where my partners and I were hunting. Suddenly the boat capsized, and the men were in the water. One couldn't swim, and he went down in deep water before my hunting partners and I could rescue him.

The first mistake these men made was in not wearing their life preservers. They had PFDs in the boat, but they were of little use.

You never know when a boating accident will occur. Wearing a personal flotation device is like an insurance policy against drowning. PFDs should always be on and zipped up when a boat is moving, and it's a good idea to wear a PFD anytime you're on the water.

Their second mistake was putting too much load into too small a boat. Little boats aren't meant for heavy loads, especially when there's a chance of encountering high waves, strong current, etc.

This lesson absolutely applies to all fishermen and other boaters. If you're going out on a big lake or river, be certain your boat is seaworthy enough to handle rough water. Sure, nobody intends to get caught in a blow, but unexpected storms can lead to disaster.

All boats are rated for maximum loads. Before you leave shore, figure the total weight that'll be in the boat, and don't overload it. Also, distribute the weight evenly throughout the boat. Don't concentrate the weight in one area.

DON'T DRINK AND BOAT. – The statistics tell a sad story. A majority of boating accidents involve alcohol consumption. Drinking and boating is just as serious as drinking and driving. (Many states now have laws against the former just as they do the latter.) The bottom line is, don't drink and boat! Also, don't ride with a boat operator who's been drinking.

AVOID KNOWN DANGER AREAS. – Tailwaters, dam intakes, rapids, waterfalls and other areas with strong currents or underwater objects pose special dangers to fishermen. Yet, some people fish these spots despite warnings to the contrary. Invariably some of them get into trouble. Never fish where posted warnings or your common-sense tells you it's unsafe. Be alert to sudden water releases when fishing below dams. After a hard rain, avoid streams prone to flash flooding.

AVOID UNSAFE ICE WHEN ICE-FISHING. – Each fall a few anglers go out on new ice too early, or in spring they try to stretch the season by fishing on ice that is thawing and rotten. Both groups are pressing their luck, and inevitably some press too far. Incidents of fishermen breaking through thin ice and drowning are all too common and could be avoided if anglers would be more cautious.

Here's the rule to follow: two inches of new, clean ice is safe to walk on. Anything less is dangerous. Also, don't walk on ice when you see air bubbles or cracks. When walking on new ice, have a partner follow a few feet behind, or you follow him! The person walking behind should carry a length of rope or a long pole to pull his partner out if he breaks through the ice. Take a long-handle chisel and tap in front of you to make sure ice is solid. But again, if there's any reasonable question that the ice is unsafe, don't go out on it!

Veteran ice fishermen follow other safety rules in the early and late season. They wear PFDs when walking on ice and carry long

Wading anglers should exercise special caution to avoid holes and dropoffs that could lead to stepping in over their heads.

Thin ice can turn an ice-fishing trip into a nightmare. Anglers should never test their luck by venturing onto ice that they have even the slightest doubt about being thick enough to support their weight.

nails or pointed dowels in a handy pocket. If you break through, these can be used to jab into ice at the edge of the hole to pull yourself out.

The Dangers of Sunburn

Sunburn rides the fence between "discomforting" and "life threatening." A sunburn is certainly uncomfortable, though the pain is only temporary. Doctors now know, however, that overexposure to the sun's ultraviolet rays can cause skin cancer, and this can be deadly.

Pro anglers used to wear shorts and fish without shirts, and they had great suntans. Today, though, most pro's have gotten the message. Many wear long pants, long-sleeved shirts, and caps with flaps to shade their ears and necks. On skin areas still exposed to the sun (back of hands, nose, cheeks), they apply a strong sunscreen.

Always apply sunscreen to exposed skin areas. Sunscreen should have an SPF (Sun Protection Factor) rating of at least 15, and 30 or higher is better. Sunscreen should be reapplied periodically when an angler is perspiring freely, since sunscreen will wash off the skin.

Overexposure to the sun's harmful rays can cause skin cancer. When fishing in bright sun, anglers should wear long-sleeve shirts and broadbrim hats to shield exposed skin. Also, they should apply sunscreen (at least SPF 15) to backs of hands, neck and other exposed areas.

The Danger of Flying Hooks

There are three times when hooks "fly:" (1) When you're casting (or when your buddy is casting); (2) when you or he snatches a hung-up lure out of a shoreside limb; (3) when you or he is fishing with a surface lure, and you set the hook and miss. These "flying" hooks can be hazardous to anglers who happen to be in their path. Be alert when you're casting, and also when others are casting. If your bait snags on a bush or limb, don't get impatient and yank. Try to flip your bait out, and if it won't come, go get it.

Sunglasses or clear safety glasses will protect your eyes from flying hooks. I wear sunglasses during daytime fishing, and I wear safety glasses when night fishing. I particularly enjoy night-fishing with topwater lures for bass. Most strikes, however, are heard instead of seen. If the fish misses the lure, and you rear back with your rod, you've got a hook-studded missile flying at you through the dark.

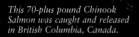

This 70-plus pound Chinook Salmon was caught and released in British Columbia, Canada.

Index